Julia Reed's New Orleans

Julia Reed's NEW ORLEANS

FOOD, FUN, AND FIELD TRIPS FOR LETTING THE GOOD TIMES ROLL

by
JULIA REED

with photographs by
PAUL COSTELLO

RIZZOLI
NEW YORK

New York Paris London Milan

contents

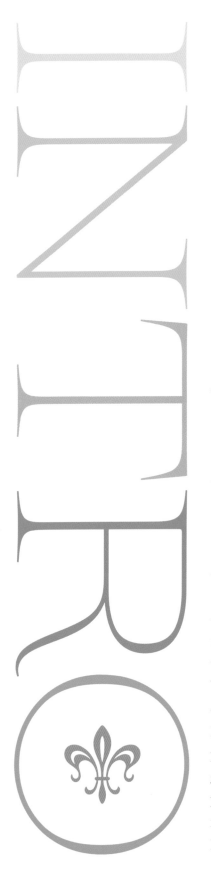

hen William Makepeace Thackeray came to New Orleans just before the Civil War, he pronounced it "the old Franco-Spanish city on the banks of the Mississippi, where, of all the cities in the world, you can eat the most and suffer the least." These days the author's assessment is more true than ever—in the aftermath of Hurricane Katrina, which devastated the city in 2005, more than 200 new restaurants have opened. But then people have always come here to eat.

As early as the 1790s, Louis Philippe was served fresh shrimp on plates of solid gold at a sugar planter's River Road plantation. Brunch is said to have been invented in New Orleans, at Madame Begue's Decatur Street establishment, which served a five- or six-course "second breakfast," complete with booze and chicory coffee to dockworkers and other early morning souls who were famished before noon. In 1840, Antoine's, now one of the country's longest-running family-owned restaurants, opened its doors and would later name oysters Rockefeller after John D. because the dish was as rich as he was. Arnaud's and Galatoire's soon followed, and all three still serve some version of Creole cooking, America's only indigenous cuisine.

The term "Creole" was applied originally to white descendants of Louisiana's first French settlers; these days it's used as an adjective to describe everything from tomatoes to cream cheese. In any event, Creole cooking is anything but pure. An amalgam of New Orleans's diverse—and ever-expanding—culture, its foundation is French (rémoulade, Bordelaise, and hollandaise sauces are still immensely popular) and African (African slaves brought over okra, gave us gumbo, replaced French chefs in homes as well as in professional kitchens). Significant contributions were also made by the Spanish, who took over the colony from the French in 1763; the Italians, who had already taught many of the French chefs in their home country thanks to Catherine de' Medici (and a huge wave of Southern Italians arrived beginning in the mid-nineteenth century); West Indian slaves, who brought exotic peppers and other ingredients; and Native Americans, whose powdered sassafras leaves were used to thicken gumbo.

Cajuns, who were granted refuge in southwest Louisiana by the Spanish, had their own separate culture and a cuisine that relied heavily on wild game and shellfish and one-pot meals such as étouffées. They in turn were influenced by German settlers, small farmers who brought with them their tradition of fine sausage making and raising and curing their own meats. In the 1970s, when Paul Prudhomme introduced his brand of Cajun cooking to New Orleans, Cajun specialties that hadn't

already appeared on Creole menus began creeping into the mix.

Post Katrina, a new round of gutsy outsiders, lured to the city by the opportunity to contribute to its culinary renaissance, has added even more energy. Tariq Hanna, who grew up in Nigeria and England, is now pastry chef and partner at Sucré, a sleek mid-century space with house-made chocolates, gelato, macaroons, and the fanciest Mardi Gras king cake in town. "We're here, all of us, to breathe new life into the culture," he says. Hanna, who had a secure post in Detroit, cashed in his 401(k), tattooed a fleur-de-lis on his arm and "never looked back." Likewise, Richard and Danielle Sutton, proprietors of the St. James Cheese Co. who met while students at Tulane, took a gamble. "Nobody had ever opened a place devoted purely to cheese in the entire Gulf region," Richard says, adding that New Orleans's traditional rich gumbos and sauces are not exactly conducive to a big cheese plate after dinner. But it turned out, he says, that the locals are "pretty adventurous."

St. James is one of the many happy poster children of post-Katrina New Orleans, a city now dotted with similar specialty food shops and new restaurants, ranging from El Gato Negro (one of the fortuitous results of the recent influx of Mexican residents) and Marjie's Grill (a crazy-good eatery inspired by Southeast Asian bar food and featuring open-fire cooking and the freshest Gulf bounty) to Turkey and the Wolf, the wildly popular sandwich joint helmed by Mason Hereford, who recently added an all-day breakfast spot, Molly's Rise and Shine, to his portfolio.

Even some of the more staid Creole standbys have benefited from the new energy. In late 2014, the long-stagnant

"We're here, all of us, to breathe new life into the culture," he says. Hanna cashed in his 401(k), tattooed a fleur-de-lis on his arm and "never looked back."

Brennan's, founded by Owen Brennan in 1946, got a stunning $20 million face-lift and a talented chef Slade Rushing, who once toiled at New York's Jack's Luxury Oyster Bar. I grew up having breakfast at Brennan's, oysters on the half shell at Felix's, raucous lunches and dinners at Galatoire's. I'm happy to report that I still do all those things—and all three establishments are mentioned in this book, which is, of course, a highly personal tome. For example, I count Donald Link and the many talented people on his and Stephen Stryjewski's team as my closest friends, so you will see them, a lot, on these pages. They also run five of the best restaurants in the country (Herbsaint, Cochon, Cochon Butcher (Butcher), Pêche, and Gianna—plus a bakery/café called La Boulangerie) so I dine at each with great frequency. I am also a lucky regular at John Harris's stellar Lilette (so lovely and light filled and delicious) as well as at his super-chic late-night bar and small-plate spot, Bouligny Tavern, next door. Then there is Coquette, where the brilliant Kristen Essig and Michael Stoltzfus consistently turn out the most innovative Southern food around (with occasional equally creative nods to classic French). Every weekend meal should include their family-style platter of mind-bogglingly good fried chicken with deviled eggs and house-made pickles, and their bread is, I swear, the best in America.

I have lived in New Orleans off and (mostly) on for almost thirty years, so a complete list of favorite haunts would be

far too long to list in this space. Suffice to say, I've put away hundreds of Pimm's Cups at the Napoleon House; I've kept more than a few hangovers at bay with a chocolate freeze and a cheeseburger from the Camellia Grill; some of my most life-changing moments have taken place on a barstool at Vaughan's; I am not averse to the late-night charms of a Lucky Dog. I have also learned a few things. I may not have cracked the code that includes the stranger customs of certain highly social Mardi Gras krewes, but that sort of arcana is not high on my list of concerns. What I do know is that the "Holy Trinity" still refers to the Father, Son, and Holy Ghost in this highly Catholic place, but also to the chopped onions, celery, and bell pepper that are the basis of so many Creole dishes. The po'boy is a near-hallowed object that supposedly earned its name in the 1920s when free sandwiches were given to striking workers dubbed "poor boys," and it is properly ordered "dressed"—meaning with mayo, lettuce, tomato, and, sometimes, pickles. People "make groceries" rather than buy them; a median is called a neutral ground, while a sidewalk is a banquette.

The po'boy is a near-hallowed object that supposedly earned its name in the 1920s when free sandwiches were given to striking workers dubbed "poor boys."

I grew up in the Mississippi Delta and we beat a path to the city pretty much every chance we got. In 1991, I came for Jazz Fest and stuck around to cover a typically crazy election. Soon enough, my French Quarter apartments got bigger and better and more magical, while New York, where I worked and owned a piece of real estate on the Upper East Side, inexorably morphed into my part-time home. In 2005, just before Katrina, I gave it up for good. During my time here, I've married and divorced; bought, renovated, sold (and wrote a book about) a lovely disaster of a house; and (hopefully) contributed in some small way to the city's recovery. As I

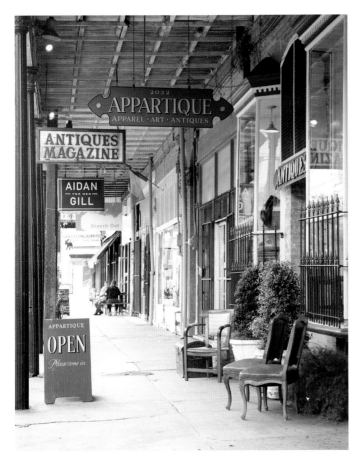

type, I am looking out my window through the branches of a hundred-year-old live oak tree at the tops of the above-ground graves in the cemetery across the street. In a minute, I'll decide where to have lunch, which will undoubtedly include an adult beverage. It's Friday, after all, and "Friday lunch" is still a sacred New Orleans institution.

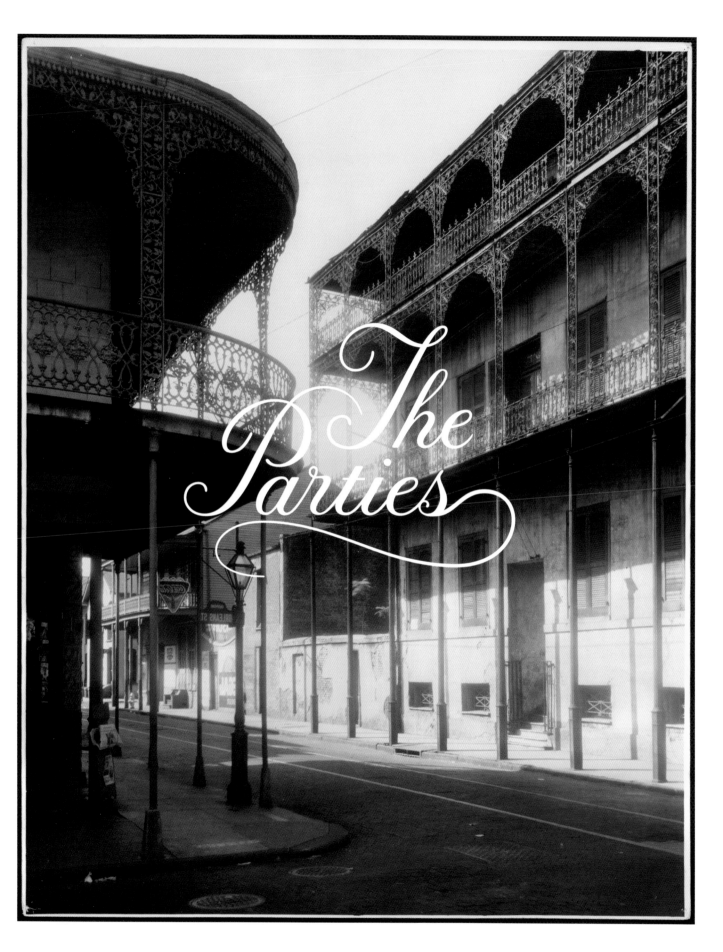

MENU

STRAWBERRY BASIL MOJITOS

ELLEN'S STRAWBERRY MIGNONETTE
with Oysters on the Half Shell

ELLEN'S STRAWBERRY SALSA
with Tortilla Chips

CRAWFISH & ANDOUILLE TART

CRAWFISH ÉTOUFFÉE

WHITE RICE

GREEN SALAD
with Judy's "French" Dressing

THE BEST BERRY COBBLER

A "Festival" of Strawberries and Crawfish

Louisiana is a state in almost perpetual festival mode: There's the New Orleans Jazz and Heritage Festival (better known as Jazz Fest), of course, and the Essence Festival, put on by the eponymous magazine, each of which draws hundreds of thousands to the city. But on a smaller scale, there are festivals to celebrate everything from Creole tomatoes, po'boys, oysters, Louisiana peaches, andouille sausage, sugarcane, and rice to Zydeco music, Swamp Pop music, alligators, "Fur and Wildlife," bonfires (right around Christmas), and Tennessee Williams, who lived for a time in the French Quarter and found his voice there. Then there's the excellently named but sadly discontinued Yambilee Festival, held in Opelousas to promote the local sweet potato crop. And there's that priceless juxtaposition, the Shrimp and Petroleum Festival, held to honor the two primary industries of Morgan City (a place which is at least as notable, to me at least, for being where Kris Kristofferson wrote "Me and Bobby McGee").

April, a month of glorious, mostly humidity-free weather, is when two of the most popular shindigs are held: the Ponchatoula Strawberry Festival and the Breaux Bridge

Crawfish Festival. The former features a parade, a king and queen who wear crowns of "ruby" strawberries embedded in the rhinestones, and an auction of the blue ribbon–winning berries. The latter is a slightly more raucous event that includes thirty Cajun bands, a ton of food stands, a crawfish-eating contest, a crawfish étouffée cook-off, a crawfish race (yes, a live crawfish race, in a round tub), and a Cajun and Zydeco dance contest.

The good news is that you can hold your own festival of both strawberries and crawfish right at home because the markets are full of both at their peak. I held mine in the gorgeous double courtyard of my next-door neighbor, the ever-generous Vaughan Fitzpatrick. We had a tiny Cajun band, tasty strawberry cocktails, and my étouffée, which is inspired by Paul Prudhomme and roux-based, though lots of folks prefer a simpler sautéed version. (As with most Cajun and Creole dishes, there are as many versions as there are cooks.) We accompanied the food with lots of rosé wine and Champagne, since the accidental theme seemed to be "Think Pink." As it happened, the dinner took place on the last night of the first weekend of Jazz Fest, so we had lots of hungry and thirsty music lovers drifting in, and a festive time was had by all.

Strawberry Basil Mojitos

2 cups white rum
2 cups Strawberry Basil Syrup
    (recipe follows)
Club soda
Strawberry halves and basil
    sprigs for garnish

I use the word "mojito" fairly loosely here, as I substitute lemon for the usual lime juice and basil for the mint. By any name, this is a refreshing cocktail that makes excellent use of the bounty of berry season. I make mine with Old New Orleans Crystal Rum, distilled from sugarcane grown in southeast Louisiana, but any good white rum will do.

In a large pitcher, stir the rum and berry syrup together to mix well. Pour into highball glasses over ice and top each one with a splash of club soda. Garnish with two or three strawberry halves and a leafy sprig of basil.

Makes about 1 quart

4 cups strawberries, washed,
    stemmed, and halved
Juice of 2 lemons
2 ¼ cups sugar
1 bunch basil

STRAWBERRY BASIL SYRUP

Place the berry halves in a large bowl and crush them using a potato masher (or pulse briefly in a food processor). Place the crushed berries in a large, heavy-bottomed pan, add the lemon juice, and bring to a boil. Reduce the heat to a simmer and cook for 25 minutes until the fruit is very soft.

Strain the mixture into a medium saucepan, pressing as much juice from the berries as possible with a ladle. Bring the mixture to a boil and add the sugar. Stir until the sugar is just dissolved.

Remove from heat and add the basil. Let steep for about 20 minutes. Remove the basil and strain the syrup into a pitcher. Any leftover syrup can be refrigerated for up to two weeks.

Ellen's Strawberry Mignonette

I have always loved mignonette sauce with oysters but sometimes the vinegar can be overpowering. The genius addition of the strawberries and sugar is the perfect foil for the acid and it gentles things up in an interesting way. Or as my dear, dear friend Ellen Stimson herself says, "The tang of vinegar next to the sweetness of strawberries and the heat of the pepper behind the brininess of the oysters, is almost too many good flavors to take in all at once. But you don't have to. Because they merge into a sweet little symphony of taste. It is a perfect bite."

Combine all ingredients in a small bowl. Serve alongside oysters.

NOTE: For diehards, I also offer a classic cocktail sauce made of ketchup, prepared horseradish, and lemon juice, along with a dash or two each of Worcestershire sauce and Tabasco. When the great Mike Rogers was the oyster shucker at the late and much-lamented Uglesich's (he now toils—and entertains—at Casamento's), he told me the secret to a perfect cocktail sauce was a few drops of olive oil. He was right.

1 tablespoon coarsely ground black peppercorns
¼ cup champagne vinegar
2 tablespoons finely chopped shallots
1 teaspoon sugar
2 tablespoons Ellen's Strawberry Salsa (recipe follows)
Sea salt, to taste

Ellen's Strawberry Salsa

4 cups strawberries

1 cucumber, seeds removed and
roughly chopped

1 jalapeño, seeds and membrane
removed (for more heat,
include a few of the seeds)

½ teaspoon salt,
or more to taste

¼ teaspoon freshly ground
pepper, or more to taste

½ to ¾ cup brown sugar,
depending on the sweetness
of the strawberries

1 bunch cilantro, chopped

NOTE: The salsa is best after it
sits for at least an hour. You can
also make it up to a day ahead
of time and keep it refrigerated
overnight.

Ellen Stimson is one of the best cooks I know and this is one of her entertaining go-tos. Whenever she throws a party in her divine farmhouse in land-locked Vermont, she flies in a pile of oysters and serves them on the half shell with an improbable strawberry mignonette that I fell in love with at first bite. Since this salsa is required for the mignonette, she always makes more than she needs and puts it out with a bowl of tortilla chips. It's so yummy that it usually disappears before the guests arrive. Try to hold out. They'll go mad for it.

Roughly chop 1 cup of strawberries and set aside.

Place the remaining ingredients in the bowl of a food processor and process until mostly smooth—you want a little texture. Stir in the chopped strawberries and serve with tortilla chips.

Crawfish & Andouille Tart

1 sheet frozen all-butter
  puff pastry

2 extra-large egg yolks

1 pound andouille sausage

2 tablespoons extra-virgin olive
  oil, plus more for drizzling

2 tablespoons butter

1 pound shelled crawfish tails

½ cup fresh goat cheese

¼ cup crème fraîche

2 teaspoons dried thyme

Kosher salt to taste

Cayenne pepper to taste

1 tablespoon snipped chives

NOTE: When cut into six bigger pieces, this makes a nice main dish. I accompany it with a green salad with lots of fresh soft herbs.

Crawfish, andouille sausage, and goat cheese turn out to have a marvelous affinity for one another. I first encountered them together in a dip my friend the fabulous Angèle Parlange used to bring to almost every party I threw, so this tart is dedicated to her.

Preheat the oven to 400°F.

Defrost the puff pastry slightly and unroll it onto a parchment-lined baking sheet. Use a short knife to score a ¼-inch border around the edge of the pastry.

In a small bowl, whisk one of the egg yolks with ¼ teaspoon of water and brush along the pastry border. Place the pastry on the baking sheet in the freezer until you are ready to use it.

Slice the andouille into thin disks (if the sausage is especially wide in diameter, cut the disks in half). In a large skillet, sauté the sausage in 1 tablespoon oil over medium heat until pleasantly browned and slightly caramelized at the edges, 3 to 4 minutes. Remove from heat, put the sausage in a medium bowl, and set aside.

Add the butter to the same skillet (don't wipe it out) over medium-low heat. Add the crawfish tails and stir to make sure all of them are well coated, about 2 minutes. Remove from heat and set aside.

Place the goat cheese, the remaining egg yolk, and the remaining tablespoon of oil in the bowl of a food processor. Puree until smooth and remove to a mixing bowl. Fold in the crème fraîche and season with 1 teaspoon of the thyme, a healthy pinch of salt, and a pinch of cayenne.

Remove the pastry from the freezer and spread the goat cheese mixture within the scored border. Arrange the andouille and the crawfish on top. You may refrigerate the tart, covered in plastic wrap, for a few hours if you're not ready to bake it.

Bake the tart for 20 to 25 minutes, rotating the baking sheet after 10 minutes, until the crust is golden brown. Sprinkle the cooked tart with the remaining teaspoon of thyme and the snipped chives. Let the tart cool for a few minutes, then transfer to a cutting board, and cut into squares. Serve on the board.

CRAWFISH FOR THE CAUSE

Crawfish season in Louisiana, which usually begins at the beginning of March and ends sometime in June, is also the season of countless backyard "boils." Requiring the same outdoor propane cooker that folks down here use to deep fry their Thanksgiving and Christmas turkeys, a boil consists of a pile of crawfish cooked with onions, potatoes, and corn. Sometimes there are whole cloves of garlic, sometimes mushrooms. Always, there is seasoning: Zatarain's, Slap Ya Mama, Swamp Fire, the cook's secret blend. When all is done, the contents of the pot get dumped on paper-covered tables and folks dig in, with plenty of cold beer at the ready.

I was given my first lesson in how to eat a boiled crawfish almost thirty years ago at Black's in Abbeville, and by now it's second nature. First, you twist and pull the tail from the head. Pause for a second to suck the head (I swear you won't be sorry), and then peel the first couple of rings of shell from around the tail. Finally, pinch the end of the tail and pull out the meat, preferably with your teeth.

Every April, I look forward to the boil put on by the Link Stryjewski Foundation, the board of which I am proud to serve on. The fundamental goal of the foundation, led by two of the coolest, smartest, most generous guys I know, chefs and partners Donald Link and Stephen Stryjewksi, is to help nourish and educate the city's youth. To that end, it provides crucial support to groups like Kingsley House and the Youth Empowerment Project that work hard to address the persistent cycle of violence and poverty affecting our young people, as well as the lack of quality education and job opportunities. We also have a blast with the kids along the way.

The foundation puts on lots of festive fundraisers throughout the year, including a fantastical Bal Masqué in January. But for pure fun and deliciousness, you can't beat Crawfish for the Kids, held on the street outside Cochon and Cochon Butcher, two of Donald and Stephen's stellar restaurants. Donald enlists his cousin Billy Link, who farms crawfish and rice in Crowley, Louisiana, and he arrives with his big rig, his eldest son, Kane, and his incredibly sweet wife, Becky. A Cajun band plays, the street fills up, and hundreds of pounds of the best crawfish I've ever tasted are consumed, washed down with multiple bottles of Miller ponies.

My new goal is to get Billy to cater a boil for me, but in the meantime, I look forward to the annual foundation shindig. When I can't get Billy's transcendent crustaceans, I head to the Big Fisherman on Magazine Street for takeout (they also pack for shipping) or I pull up a chair at the divine Marjie's Grill on Broad Street—they do magical things with mudbugs every day of the season.

LINK STRYJEWSKI FOUNDATION
linkstryjewski.org
BIG FISHERMAN SEAFOOD
3301 Magazine Street, bigfishermanseafood.com
MARJIE'S GRILL
320 South Broad Street, marjiesgrill.com

ALL PROCEEDS
BENEFIT
LINK STRYJEWSKI
FOUNDATION
&
NEW ORLEANS
YOUTH

Crawfish Étouffée

This dish is one of my very favorites to make. It is rich (believe me when I say that the stick of butter at the end is highly necessary), easy (the tails come already shelled in a vacuum-sealed bag and I use store-bought seafood stock), and hugely popular. The recipe was inspired by my Cajun cooking guru, the late, great Paul Prudhomme. Nobody understood how to create depths of flavor and heat better, and nobody was kinder or more generous. He did not add Cognac or Worcestershire to his étouffée, but both seem to smooth out the flavors and add that all-important umami. Sometimes I add a squeeze of lemon, too. And don't forget to have some warm French bread and a bottle of hot sauce on the table.

In a small bowl, thoroughly blend the first six ingredients to create a seasoning mix and set aside. (You may not need all of the mix. Any leftovers can be stored in a sealed jar at room temperature.)

In a large, heavy-bottomed saucepan or Dutch oven, heat the oil over high heat until it begins to smoke, about 4 minutes. Gradually whisk in the flour, stirring constantly to keep from scorching. Make sure to eliminate any lumps and keep whisking for 3 to 5 minutes, until the roux turns a medium reddish brown.

Dump in the chopped vegetables and remove from heat. Stir in 1 tablespoon of seasoning mix and keep stirring, off heat, until the vegetables have softened a bit, about 3 minutes. Return the pan to heat, slowly whisk in the stock, and bring to a boil. Lower to simmer, whisk in tomato paste, and cook for 25 minutes. Remove from heat.

In a large skillet or saucepan, melt 1 stick of the butter. Add the crawfish and scallions and stir constantly until the crawfish is coated and the onions are wilted, 2 to 3 minutes.

Return the roux mixture to medium heat and stir in the crawfish mixture. Stir in the Cognac and a couple of generous dashes of Worcestershire sauce. Add the remaining stick of butter and a scant tablespoon of seasoning mix and stir until the butter melts.

Serve immediately over hot white rice. This dish can also be made a day or two ahead of time and gently reheated.

2 teaspoons salt

2 teaspoons cayenne pepper

1 teaspoon white pepper

1 teaspoon freshly ground black pepper

1 teaspoon dried basil

1 teaspoon dried thyme

¼ cup plus 3 tablespoons vegetable oil

¾ cup all-purpose flour

¼ cup chopped onion

¼ cup chopped celery

¼ cup chopped green bell pepper

3 cups seafood stock

2 tablespoons tomato paste

2 sticks butter

2 pounds peeled crawfish tails

1 cup sliced scallions, including the tender green parts

¼ cup Cognac

Lea & Perrins Worcestershire sauce to taste

Cooked white rice

NOTE: I have made this dish for as many as eighty people (ten times the recipe) with no problem. Just be extra sure not to multiply the peppers in the seasoning mix, a lesson I learned the hard way. The trick, as for all "stewy" dishes—whether you make them for eight or for eighty—is to taste and taste again.

Green Salad with Judy's "French" Dressing

FOR THE DRESSING

1 ½ cups oil (I use 1 cup vegetable, safflower, or canola oil with ½ cup olive oil, as a dressing made with only olive oil is too heavy for my taste)

½ cup red wine vinegar

½ cup sugar

2 teaspoons curry powder

½ white onion, sliced

Juice of 1 lemon

½ teaspoon salt

Pinch of cayenne pepper

½ teaspoon Lea & Perrins Worcestershire sauce

FOR THE SALAD

4 cups romaine leaves, torn

4 cups red leaf lettuce leaves, torn

1 head endive, trimmed and cut into 2-inch pieces

1 bunch scallions or 2 shallots, sliced

1 cup hearts of palm, sliced

6 to 8 radishes, sliced

With the rich étouffée and rice, something crisp and green is definitely called for. So is the tang of my mother's "French" dressing. A sort of gourmet riff on those once-ubiquitous bottles of Kraft French, this dressing has been in my mother's repertoire since she arrived in her first kitchen, newly married and with a notebook full of recipes from my grandmother's cook and my aunt Frances, who had been to cooking school. It is one of my very favorites. The sugar and the hint of curry (nobody can ever figure out what exactly it is) provide the perfect counterpoint to the slight heat of the crawfish. You will have lots left over, but it will keep for a couple of weeks in the fridge. As for the salad, go with what you like. Here, I use a mix of romaine, red leaf, and endive leaves, but I often go with the more basic combo of romaine and iceberg. The radishes add another pop of red and some crunch, and I'm a sucker for hearts of palm.

For the dressing, mix all ingredients together. (I usually make like Mama and throw everything in a big Mason jar and shake.) Cover and refrigerate for at least 24 hours. Before using, let the dressing come to room temperature and remove the onion slices. Leftovers will keep at least a couple of weeks in the refrigerator.

For the salad, mix all the ingredients in a large salad bowl. Toss with about ½ cup of the dressing, but add the dressing slowly, taking care not to drown the greens—you can always add more if needed. Taste for salt and serve.

The Best
Berry Cobbler

This cobbler is loosely adapted from *Chez Panisse Desserts,* an indispensable tome by the brilliant Lindsay Shere, and is as easy as it is delicious. I usually make it with a combo of blackberries and blueberries, but in honor of the season (and our menu), this one includes strawberries mixed with raspberries (plus a little orange juice and zest) for flavor and texture. In New Orleans, I accompany it with Creole cream cheese ice cream, which is made by both the New Orleans Ice Cream Co. and Blue Bell Creameries, but vanilla ice cream or whipped cream would be almost as good.

Preheat the oven to 375ºF.

In a large bowl, toss the berries with the orange juice, 1/3 cup of the sugar, and 2 tablespoons of the flour and set aside.

In a large bowl, mix together the remaining 1 1/2 cups flour, the salt, the remaining 1 1/2 tablespoons of sugar, the baking powder, and the orange zest. Cut in the butter with two forks or a pastry blender until the mixture looks like coarse cornmeal. (I usually end up using my hands but you can also use a food processor.) Add the cream and mix until the mixture is just moistened and comes together. Shape the dough into patties, about 2 inches in diameter and 1/2 inch thick.

Put the berry mixture in a 1 1/2 - or 2-quart gratin or baking dish. Arrange the dough patties on top of the berries. Bake for 45 minutes until the patties are brown and the berry juice bubbles around them.

Let cool slightly and serve straight from the dish accompanied by ice cream or whipped cream.

4 cups strawberries, halved
2 cups raspberries
1 tablespoon freshly squeezed orange juice
1/3 cup plus 1 1/2 tablespoons sugar
2 tablespoons plus 1 1/2 cups all-purpose flour
Scant 1/2 teaspoon salt
2 1/4 teaspoons baking powder
2 teaspoons grated orange zest
6 tablespoons unsalted butter, cut into 12 pieces
3/4 cup heavy cream
Ice cream or whipped cream

Restaurant Tribute

T

This menu is my homage to the city's great temples of Creole cuisine—Antoine's, Arnaud's, and Galatoire's—located within blocks of each other in the French Quarter and founded at least one hundred years ago by French immigrants. When I was a kid, fine dining in New Orleans meant dining at one of those three spots, period, with occasional side trips to Felix's oyster bar, whose proximity to Galatoire's meant that you could slurp down a dozen raw while someone held your place in line in front of the restaurant. (Galatoire's has since added an upstairs bar, which means that the fabled and always festive line—formed because the downstairs dining room does not take reservations—is no longer.)

There was Brennan's, too, founded in 1946 after "Count" Arnaud told Owen Brennan that Irishmen couldn't do French food, and where breakfast at Brennan's was the thing. After Ella Brennan took over Commander's Palace in 1974, it joined the pantheon.

Brennan's recently has been reinvigorated by Ralph Brennan, who oversaw a gorgeous renovation and brought in the talented chef Slade Rushing. And Commander's still thrives with Ella's daughter, Ti Martin, and niece, Lally Brennan, at the helm. Restaurants all over town—ranging from Brigtsen's (owned by Commander's alum Frank Brigtsen) to Upperline to Donald Link's Herbsaint—now offer inventive interpretations of Creole cuisine. But the three temples still stand, dishing out thousands of orders of soufflé potatoes (fried puffed potatoes) each week along with countless dozens of oysters Rockefeller (invented at Antoine's) and oysters Bienville (created by Arnaud), followed by flaming copper bowls of café brulöt. Each shows varying signs of wear and tear, and each often serves lackluster food. But all three are hugely popular with locals and tourists alike, and all three can be a ton of fun.

I've had countless lunches that have spilled into dinner (I think my record is eight hours, but I am hardly alone in that achievement).

Antoine's, established in 1840 by Antoine Alciatore, is by far the oldest of the three as well as the originator of such Creole standards as pompano en papillote, oysters Foch, and eggs Sardou, in addition to the famous Rockefeller, Jules Alciatore's riff on escargot using the far more plentiful Gulf oysters. Some of the most romantic lunches of my life have taken place in the main dining room during the Christmas season, when it is lit primarily by the lights on the colorful tree. I've given memorable dinners in the Mystery Room, where the red walls lend themselves to masses of crimson roses down the long table, and I've been a lucky guest at the extremely raucous lunches hosted by the Krewe of Proteus, which takes over the entire restaurant on the Monday before Mardi Gras.

At the sprawling Arnaud's, opened in 1918 by French wine salesman Arnaud Cazenave, my favorite spot is the dark and elegant French 75 bar, where a superb version of the namesake cocktail is on offer and the hors d'oeuvres include soufflé potatoes (the best version in town) and deviled eggs. What more, really, does one need?

But it is at Galatoire's, founded in 1905 by Jean Galatoire, that I am a true regular, where I've had countless lunches that have spilled into dinner (I think my record is eight hours, but I am hardly alone in that achievement), where I've celebrated big birthdays and small victories, where I've loved and lost waiters (the late great Cesar once got so sick of my indecision as to what to order—it was at the end of a very busy Sunday—that he walked down the street and bought a bag of Krystal burgers, which he plopped down on my table before departing). These days, my waiter is most often Billy, who knows as soon as he sees my face to bring over a martini on the rocks accompanied by what I call the "martini salad," a small bowl overflowing with cocktail onions, lemon twists, and both pimento-stuffed and anchovy-stuffed olives. Before Billy, I was well tended by his father, Harold, the soul of Cajun bonhomie, and Bryant, his first cousin. When he's not around, I love Ruchelle, daughter-in-law of one of my favorite maître d's, Arnold Chabaud. All are examples of the family connections and long histories that both the staff and the clientele maintain. I know my well-being will soar the moment I walk in the door and Joe Plavetsky (who knows more about wine than anyone I know) takes me by the hand to lead me to my table.

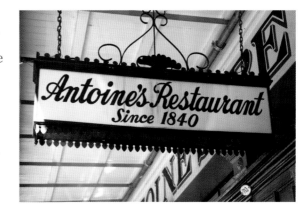

If you order carefully at Galatoire's, you can eat really well, and your waiter is always your best guide. (There is a menu but I have yet to actually look at it.) He or she will tell you what fish is freshest and what dish is definitely not up to snuff. My mainstays are shrimp Yvonne (a sauté of shrimp, artichoke hearts, and mushrooms that is named after the Galatoire family matriarch who manned the desk for the first half of my life), the best crawfish étouffée in town (but only in season), crabmeat canapé (a perfect mound of crabmeat bound only by a light béchamel and baked on a round piece of toast), and thick, perfectly broiled lamb chops. There is also the famous Grand Goute platter featuring shrimp rémoulade, crabmeat maison, some additional iteration of cold shrimp or crawfish, and fried oysters en brochette wrapped in crispy bacon.

A few years ago, I continued with my just-ordered dinner after a bomb threat was phoned in to Galatoire's and all the other diners had been quietly asked to leave—which they did with some alacrity. I had no intention of budging since, in the

first place, I was highly doubtful that a bomb was actually in the vicinity (the call turned out to have been made by a dishwasher who had been fired the day before), and in the second place, if such an event were in fact to happen, I was damn sure going to stick around to be a witness. The evening ended up being a rather different sort of blast, with all the waiters and the busboys sitting down to enjoy the abandoned food and wine, a party that finally moved next door to Larry Flynt's newly opened strip club (to celebrate the birthday of one of the managers).

Not every night in any of the three spots is quite as exciting, but they are all worthy of celebration. They made New Orleans a culinary capital early on in the city's history and continue to provide sustenance and

safe haven to loyal diners. One of my own frequent dining companions at Galatoire's, where we have long, Champagne-fueled lunches, is Patrick Dunne, a dear friend and the owner of Lucullus, the culinary antiques store on Chartres Street that is by now as revered as the restaurants themselves. Patrick, too, lives in a Creole temple of sorts—a seriously gorgeous, antiques-filled town house in the Faubourg Marigny. As soon as I step inside, I'm transported to the era of Antoine Alciatore himself. I could think of no better place to host this dinner than in Patrick's dining room, where we ate off period French porcelain plates and toasted our city's culinary history and our own great good fortune with Patrick's heavy French glasses.

To take the lead in Patrick's seductive, copper-filled kitchen, I enlisted Taylor Haxton, the son of my closest friend and a dear and smart and funny young man who has made a name for himself in New Orleans kitchens ranging from Herbsaint to Restaurant R'evolution. Among the diners was Cedric Martin, another great pal who is proprietor of Martin Wine Cellar, founded by his father in 1946, and where I got the swell Bordeaux we had with our beef. To entertain us all, Patrick was thoughtful enough to ask the talented Stefan Poole to play the saxophone during the cocktail hour. It was a magical New Orleans night.

Patrick's Sazerac

NOTE: To make the simple syrup in Patrick's recipe, bring 1 cup of raw sugar (turbinado) and 1 cup of water to a boil over high heat. Cook, stirring occasionally, until the sugar is completely dissolved, about 5 minutes. Allow to cool, and store in the refrigerator for up to two weeks.

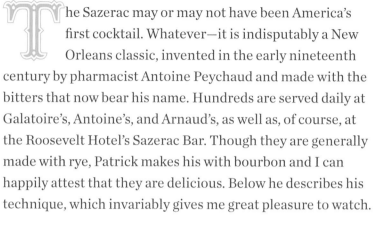

The Sazerac may or may not have been America's first cocktail. Whatever—it is indisputably a New Orleans classic, invented in the early nineteenth century by pharmacist Antoine Peychaud and made with the bitters that now bear his name. Hundreds are served daily at Galatoire's, Antoine's, and Arnaud's, as well as, of course, at the Roosevelt Hotel's Sazerac Bar. Though they are generally made with rye, Patrick makes his with bourbon and I can happily attest that they are delicious. Below he describes his technique, which invariably gives me great pleasure to watch.

"For me, mixing a cocktail is not unlike making love: It's never the same and easily spoils if overwrought. My minimal bartending skills were initially learned under pressure at the knee of my grandfather, who was both fastidious and impatient. Critical is the glass. Only a high-sided, old—yes, an *old* tumbler with deep fluting to allow for a decent grip—will do. Pour a small puddle of Herbsaint, the size of a pearl earring, into the glass. Then, depending on the steadiness of the hand and the absence of silk dresses nearby, toss high and spin in the air to coat the inside of the tumbler and then set aside. Into a tall glass, pour 3 masculine dashes of Peychaud's bitters to which is added in this sequence: Instead of a sugar cube, a goodly dash of simple syrup made at home of brown Louisiana cane sugar; then a generous dose of bourbon (not rye). All is stirred vigorously with a silver spoon over 2 ice cubes—more ice would water the drink. Strain into the tumbler with an ample-size lemon peel pinched over the drink to impart essence but no pulp.

"Bourbon was the standard ingredient for every drink at my grandfather's elbow. I'm not sure if it was more readily available or a taste preference or a stubborn Southernism. Rye, he thought bitter, Northern, and suitable for medicine. We children drank it in hot lemonade when we had the croup. I cannot find anyone who remembers the brand of bourbon he drank, and it always came out of a decanter so God knows what it was. For myself, I use Colonel E. H. Taylor small batch, which seems just fine."

Crawfish Cardinale Tarts

Crawfish Cardinale, a creamy, Cognac-tinged concoction, is a staple at Antoine's, where it is served in a ramekin. Emeril Lagasse and John Folse serve theirs as an appetizer or main course in puff pastry patty shells. For this party, I passed around a tinier taste of the rich crawfish in hors d'oeuvre–size puff pastry shells straight out of the freezer case.

Melt the butter in a large skillet over medium heat. Lower heat and add shallots and garlic, stirring often to make sure the garlic does not burn, and cook until soft, 8 to 10 minutes. Stir in the stock and tomato paste and cook 1 minute. Sprinkle in flour and cook 2 minutes, stirring constantly.

Add cream, Cognac, lemon juice, salt, and cayenne. Blend well and cook about 5 minutes, until a thickish, saucelike consistency is achieved, stirring frequently. Add the crawfish tails and cook until the tails are hot, 2 to 3 minutes more.

Remove the mixture from the heat and taste for seasonings. Spoon into the shells and serve immediately.

4 tablespoons (½ stick) butter

½ cup minced shallots

2 teaspoons minced garlic

2 tablespoons seafood stock

2 tablespoons tomato paste

2 tablespoons all-purpose flour

2 cups heavy cream

2 tablespoons Cognac or brandy

1 tablespoon freshly squeezed lemon juice

½ teaspoon salt

½ teaspoon cayenne pepper

1 pound crawfish tails

2 dozen mini pastry shells (I most often use Athens brand mini shells, which are ready to use straight out of the freezer, or Siljans crispy shells)

Judy's Fried Eggplant with Galatoire's "Table" Sauce

Serves 6 to 8 as hors doeuvres

1 tablespoon salt,
    plus more for sprinkling
1 large eggplant, peeled and
    sliced crosswise into slices
    no more than ¼ inch thick
1 sleeve Ritz crackers, unopened
    (or more, as needed)
3 large eggs, beaten
Vegetable oil

My mother has never met a Ritz cracker she didn't like. She uses them, crushed and buttered, on top of more casseroles than I can count, and the same crushed crackers replace cornmeal when she fries green tomatoes or eggplant. I much prefer her thin-sliced disks of eggplant to Galatoire's sticks, which are coated in Italian bread crumbs. What I do like at Galatoire's is the accidental sauce concocted during one heavily lubricated dinner by my ex-husband, John Pearce, at our table. Because eggplant sometimes can be bitter (a problem eliminated by the salt soak below), it has long been a tradition at the restaurant to serve the sticks accompanied by bowls of powdered sugar. (They also serve them with béarnaise sauce, which I occasionally do as well.) John has done a whole lot of good things in his life, but the creation of this sauce was, I have to say, one of his more inspired moments. He simply took the Tabasco that was already on the table, along with the wine at hand, and whipped up the perfect mix of sweet and hot that happens to go brilliantly with the eggplant. These days, you see tables all over the dining room doing the same thing.

Fill a large bowl with ice water and add the salt. Stir to blend and then add the eggplant slices. Soak for about an hour.

Meanwhile crush the Ritz crackers by wrapping the unopened sleeve in a dish towel and beating it with a rolling pin. You can also place the crackers in the bowl of a food processor and pulse a couple of times for a finer texture. (Mama likes hers fairly coarse and I do, too.)

Drain the eggplant and dry thoroughly. Dip each slice in beaten egg to coat well and dredge in cracker crumbs, pressing to make sure they adhere. Transfer onto a rimmed baking sheet lined with paper towels.

Heat about 2 inches of oil in a large skillet over medium-high heat until very hot. (It should be around 375°F. If you don't have a thermometer, stick the handle of a wooden spoon into the oil. When the oil starts steadily bubbling around the handle, you are ready to go.) Fry the eggplant in batches (do not crowd the pan) until golden brown, 1 to 2 minutes per side. Add more oil as needed.

Drain on paper towels and sprinkle with salt. Serve with the Galatoire's "Table" Sauce (recipe follows).

GALATOIRE'S "TABLE" SAUCE

Sift the sugar through a fine strainer to eliminate any lumps. Whisk in the Tabasco sauce and the wine or Champagne and serve.

Makes 1 cup

¾ cup confectioners' sugar
3 tablespoons Tabasco sauce
1 tablespoon white wine or Champagne

Crabmeat Ravigote

1 pound jumbo lump crabmeat

1 cup mayonnaise, preferably
   homemade

2 teaspoons Dijon mustard

2 teaspoons lemon juice

¼ teaspoon cayenne pepper

¼ teaspoon kosher salt

¼ cup capers, drained and
   minced

2 tablespoons finely chopped
   scallions

2 tablespoons finely chopped
   green bell pepper

2 tablespoons minced anchovies

1 tablespoon finely chopped
   Italian parsley

1 tablespoon finely chopped
   fresh tarragon leaves
   (optional)

For years my go-to cold crabmeat salad was the straightforward but luscious version served at Galatoire's, that is called, simply, crabmeat maison and made with mayonnaise, chopped scallions, capers, and chopped parsley. Not long ago, I had crabmeat ravigote at Antoine's and realized why *ravigoter* means "to invigorate" in French. I went home straightaway to try and duplicate it and am now a big fan of this more intensely seasoned recipe. It also reminds me very fondly of the version of crabmeat maison my late, great waiter Cesar used to bring to me at Galatoire's: piled onto saltine crackers and topped with anchovies and a lashing of cayenne pepper.

Place the crabmeat in a colander and pick it over for shells, taking care not to break up the lumps. Set aside.

In a large bowl, mix the remaining ingredients. Gently fold in the crabmeat.

NOTE: If not serving immediately, cover the crabmeat with plastic wrap and refrigerate, but this dish is absolutely best served on the same day. Here, I put it on a bed of iceberg lettuce along with Shrimp in White Rémoulade (recipe follows).

Shrimp in White Rémoulade

Serves 8 as an appetizer

FOR THE RÉMOULADE SAUCE

1 cup mayonnaise, preferably homemade

2 tablespoons Creole mustard

2 tablespoons prepared horse-radish

1 tablespoon freshly squeezed lemon juice

1 tablespoon minced Italian parsley

4 finely chopped scallions

¼ teaspoon cayenne pepper

¼ teaspoon white pepper

Kosher salt to taste

FOR THE SHRIMP

3 quarts water

1 bag Zatarain's Crawfish, Shrimp, and Crab Boil

2 tablespoons salt

2 lemons, quartered

2 pounds (16 to 20 count per pound) shrimp, unpeeled

In my previous cookbook, I included a recipe for shrimp rémoulade that has two different kinds of mustard, paprika, and even a healthy dose of ketchup. Galatoire's serves a version of red rémoulade, but the restaurant also offers up a white version that is tossed with either shrimp or crawfish tails on their Grand Goute platter. Below is my slightly altered version of their white rémoulade with shrimp.

TO MAKE THE RÉMOULADE SAUCE

In a large bowl, mix all ingredients.

TO MAKE THE SHRIMP

Combine water, crab boil, salt, and lemons in a large stockpot or Dutch oven and bring to a boil over high heat. Reduce the heat and simmer for 5 minutes. Return the heat to high and add the shrimp. Cook, uncovered, for 3 minutes. (After about 2 minutes, pluck a shrimp from the water, run it under cold water, and taste. You only want to cook them until they are no longer transparent in the center, but only just. My pet peeve is even a slightly overcooked shrimp.). Immediately dump the shrimp into a colander, discarding the seasoning bag and lemon pieces.

As soon as the shrimp are cool enough to handle, peel and place them in a large bowl. Refrigerate until ready to use.

TO ASSEMBLE THE DISH

Gently fold the cooked shrimp into the Rémoulade Sauce and taste for salt.

Fillets of Beef with Sauce Béarnaise and Sauce Médoc

Serves 8

At Galatoire's, the delicious thick-cut fillet of beef comes with a bowl of room-temperature Béarnaise that seems somehow devoid of both butter and egg yolks, not to mention salt. At Antoine's, the accompanying marchand de vin sauce is even more disappointing, resembling as it does a brown sludge. Both are great ideas and classic pairings—it's just the execution that's off or just plain lazy. Fortunately, both sauces are not hard to do really well. Julia Child's blender Béarnaise is so easy that she rightly describes it as "within the capabilities of an 8-year-old child." The great French chef Georges Perrier, whose late and much lamented Philadelphia restaurant Le Bec-Fin was among my favorites, makes a ridiculously delicious wine sauce that's also easy to make now that good demiglace is so readily available. Be sure and get the best meat you can find and don't overcook it. Then go over-the-top by accompanying it with both of these yummy sauces.

TO MAKE THE SAUCE BÉARNAISE

Bring the vinegar, wine, scallions, and 1 tablespoon of the tarragon leaves to a boil in a small saucepan over high heat. Lower heat to medium and cook until the liquid has been reduced to 2 tablespoons. Let cool.

Cut the butter into pieces and heat to foaming hot in a small saucepan. Remove from heat.

Place the vinegar mixture, salt, cayenne, and egg yolks in the jar of an electric blender and blend at top speed for 2 seconds. Still at top speed, start pouring in the hot butter in a thin stream of droplets. By the time two-thirds of the butter has been added, the sauce will be a thick cream. Finish adding the butter, omitting the milky residue at the bottom of the pan. Stir in the remaining 2 tablespoons of minced tarragon. If not serving immediately, place the blender jar in a pan of tepid water.

Makes 1 ½ cups

FOR THE SAUCE BÉARNAISE

¼ cup white wine vinegar

¼ cup dry white wine

1 tablespoon minced scallions

3 tablespoons minced fresh tarragon leaves

8 tablespoons (1 stick) of butter

¼ teaspoon salt

⅛ teaspoon cayenne pepper

3 large egg yolks

TO MAKE THE SAUCE MÉDOC

Heat the butter and oil in a large, heavy-bottomed saucepan over medium heat. Lower heat slightly and add the shallots, celery, bay leaf, mushrooms, thyme, and peppercorns. Cook until browned, 5 to 8 minutes, stirring occasionally.

Add the wine and sugar and cook for 2 minutes. Ignite the mixture with a long match. When the flames subside, add the demiglace and cook until the sauce is reduced by half. Strain the sauce through a fine sieve and set aside.

TO MAKE THE BEEF

Season the beef with salt and pepper. In each of two heavy-bottomed sauté pans or skillets, heat 1 tablespoon of the oil and 1 tablespoon of butter over medium high heat until sizzling. Add four fillets to each pan or skillet and sauté until well browned on both sides. (I cook them about 2 minutes on each side for rare and a little longer for medium rare. Perrier says he can tell that the beef is a perfect medium rare when beads of red juice appear on the surface.)

Remove the fillets from the pans or skillets, keeping them warm on a plate. Pour off the fat from the pans or skillets and deglaze each one with ¼ cup of the wine. (At this point, I would pour the wine from one pan or skillet into the other and proceed using a single skillet.)

Add the Sauce Médoc and allow the liquid to reduce until it lightly coats the spoon. Beat in the remaining butter and season with salt and pepper. Pour any juices on the plate of fillets back into the sauce.

To serve, you may either pass the Sauce Médoc separately at the table with the Sauce Béarnaise. Or you may do as I do here and place the fillets on large dinner plates, ladling a small amount of Sauce Médoc on one side and an equal amount of Béarnaise on the other (then I pass both sauces at the table, too). Either way, serve the fillets immediately.

Makes 1 ¾ cups

FOR THE SAUCE MÉDOC

1 tablespoon unsalted butter

1 tablespoon olive oil

10 shallots, sliced

2 ribs of celery, sliced

1 bay leaf

5 button mushrooms, sliced

3 sprigs fresh thyme

*½ teaspoon crushed
    black peppercorns*

*½ bottle (1 ½ cups)
    red Bordeaux wine*

½ teaspoon sugar

*2 cups demiglace (see
    Sources on page 218)*

FOR THE BEEF

*Eight 6- to 7-ounce center-cut
    fillets*

Salt to taste

White pepper to taste

2 tablespoons olive oil

6 tablespoons butter

½ cup red Bordeaux wine

"Rockefeller" Spinach

Serves 8

Salt to taste

Four 10-ounce bags
   baby spinach

4 tablespoons (½ stick) butter

4 shallots, finely chopped

3 cloves garlic, minced

2 tablespoons all-purpose flour

1 ½ cups heavy cream

3 tablespoons Pernod

¾ teaspoon salt

1 teaspoon white pepper

NOTE: You can make this up to a few hours ahead of time and reheat in the top a double boiler

Like Arnaud's and Antoine's, Galatoire's has always featured creamed spinach on its menu, but you can also order what the waiters call "Rockefeller" Spinach, which is the same dark-green Pernod-infused topping that is served on the restaurant's oysters Rockefeller. Here, I've come up with what is essentially a combination of the two.

Fill a large pot or Dutch oven about ¾ full of water. Add a generous pinch of salt and bring to a boil over high heat. Add spinach, cook 2 minutes, and dump into a colander. Rinse under cold running water until chilled. Press to extract most of the water and roughly chop.

Melt the butter in a large saucepan over low heat. Add the shallots and garlic and cook, stirring frequently, until soft, 5 to 8 minutes. Sprinkle in the flour, stir to mix well, and cook for 2 minutes. Pour in the cream, stirring all the while, and add the Pernod, salt, and pepper. Cook until slightly thickened, about 5 minutes.

Add the spinach and stir to blend. Cook until the spinach is heated through, about 5 more minutes. Taste for seasoning and serve immediately.

Brabant Potatoes

Brabant potatoes, a staple on the Galatoire's menu, are basically diced French fries unless you take them to the next level with hot garlic butter. Finished with flaky sea salt and glistening with bits of parsley, they are things of beauty—as well as the all-important crispy foil to the fillet and its sauces.

Bring 3 quarts water to a boil with a generous pinch of kosher salt in a large pot or Dutch oven over high heat. Add the diced potatoes and cook until barely fork-tender, 5 to 7 minutes. Drain in a colander.

Line two large rimmed sheet pans with paper towels. Heat 1 inch of oil in a large, heavy-bottomed skillet over medium-high heat. Add the potatoes in one layer (you will have to do this in two or three batches) and sprinkle generously with salt and pepper. Fry the potatoes, occasionally shaking the skillet back and forth and turning the potatoes often, until they are golden brown and crisp, about 12 minutes. (Add more oil as needed.) Drain the potatoes on the towel-lined pans. (At this point, you could place the sheet pans in a low oven or simply set aside for about 10 minutes while you prepare the fillets. When ready to serve, proceed to the next step. The hot butter will warm the potatoes.)

Wipe out the skillet and melt the butter over medium heat. Add the garlic and parsley, and cook, stirring constantly, about 1 minute. Add the drained potatoes, and toss to coat. Remove from heat, add the Maldon salt and more pepper to taste, and toss again. Serve immediately.

Kosher salt to taste

8 large white potatoes, peeled and cut into 1/2-inch dice

Vegetable or canola oil for frying

Freshly ground black pepper to taste

8 tablespoons (1 stick) butter

3 tablespoons minced garlic

1/4 cup minced Italian parsley

Maldon sea salt, or similar flaky finishing salt

Meringue Shells
with Coffee Ice Cream &
Orange-Chocolate Sauce

Serves 8

This dessert combines elements of Antoine's famous meringue-coated baked Alaska (which comes out of the kitchen, flaming, with much fanfare) and the almond-topped chocolate sundae at Galatoire's, which for years was the only dessert on offer other than "cup custard." At all three of the Creole temples (Antoine's, Arnaud's, and Galatoire's), dessert is often accompanied by café brulöt, strong coffee flavored with orange peel, brandy, and orange liqueur (among other flavorings, including a stick of cinnamon, depending on the restaurant) and prepared tableside in a copper bowl. The coffee ice cream and the orange-chocolate sauce are nods to that dramatic elixir (sometimes called café brulöt diabolique), albeit decidedly less dangerous. A slightly doddering waiter at Galatoire's once set our tablecloth on fire as he flamed the long corkscrew of orange peel.

Makes 8 meringue shells

**FOR THE
MERINGUE SHELLS**

*6 large egg whites, at room
    temperature*

¼ teaspoon cream of tartar

¼ teaspoon kosher salt

1 ½ cups sugar

1 teaspoon pure vanilla extract

TO MAKE THE MERINGUE SHELLS

Preheat the oven to 200°F. Line two baking sheets with parchment paper. Using a 3-inch pastry ring or a glass as a template, trace eight circles on the paper 2 inches apart.

In the bowl of an electric mixer fitted with the whisk attachment, beat the egg whites, cream of tartar, and salt on medium speed until frothy. Add 1 cup of the sugar and raise the speed to high, beating until the egg whites form very stiff peaks. Whisk in the vanilla. Carefully fold the remaining ½ cup of sugar into the meringue.

Fill a pastry bag fitted with a large star-shaped tip and pipe a disk of meringue inside each circle. Pipe two rings atop one another around the edge of each disk to form the sides of the shells. (You can also do this using a large Ziploc bag with a corner snipped off—the shells will taste just as good, they just won't be fluted.)

Bake for 2 hours, or until the meringues are dry and crisp but

not remotely browned. Turn off the heat and allow the meringues to completely cool in the oven, about 2 hours. (Ina Garten leaves hers in as long as overnight.)

Store in an airtight container for up to 2 weeks.

FOR THE
TOASTED ALMONDS

1 tablespoon butter

1 cup blanched sliced almonds

1 teaspoon fine sea salt

TO MAKE THE TOASTED ALMONDS

Preheat oven to 375°F. In a small saucepan, melt the butter over medium heat until foaming and then remove from heat. Add the almonds and stir to coat. Sprinkle in the salt and stir again.

Spread out on a rimmed baking sheet and bake until golden brown, 5 to 8 minutes, shaking pan and stirring almonds about halfway through. Remove from the oven and cool completely before using.

Makes about 3 cups

FOR THE ORANGE-
CHOCOLATE SAUCE

3 wide strips orange zest

⅔ cup cocoa powder, sifted

⅔ cup light corn syrup

1 cup water

8 ounces roughly chopped
  bittersweet chocolate

2 tablespoons butter,
  cut into 4 pieces

3 tablespoons orange-flavored
  liqueur (I prefer Cointreau)

Pinch of kosher salt

8 scoops coffee ice cream

TO MAKE THE ORANGE-CHOCOLATE SAUCE

Bring the orange zest, cocoa powder, corn syrup, and water to a boil in a medium, heavy-bottomed saucepan over high heat. Reduce heat to medium and cook, whisking constantly, for 2 minutes.

Remove from heat, discard orange zest, and stir in chocolate. Let stand a couple of minutes, and then whisk sauce until the chocolate is melted and the sauce is smooth. Add butter and whisk until fully incorporated. Whisk in liqueur and salt and serve.

NOTE: The sauce may be made up to a week ahead of time and refrigerated. Reheat slowly on the stovetop or in a microwave, where you should stir every 10 seconds until the sauce is just warm and pourable.

TO ASSEMBLE THE DESSERT

Just before serving, place one scoop of ice cream in each meringue shell. Spoon warm sauce over the ice cream and sprinkle with almonds. Serve immediately.

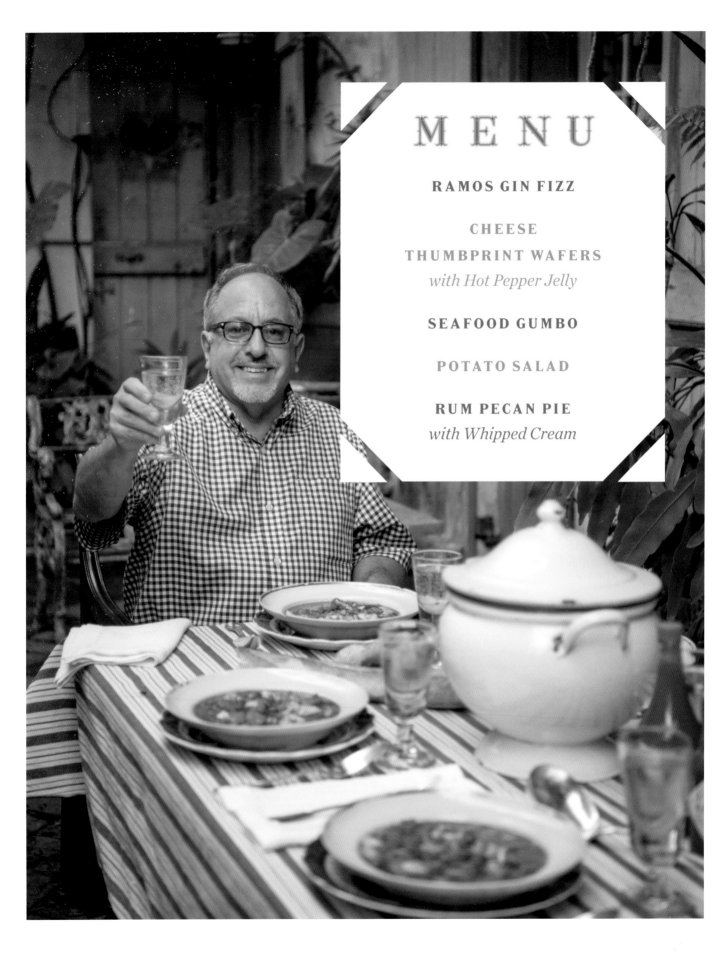

MENU

RAMOS GIN FIZZ

**CHEESE
THUMBPRINT WAFERS**
with Hot Pepper Jelly

SEAFOOD GUMBO

POTATO SALAD

RUM PECAN PIE
with Whipped Cream

GUMBO Lunch

In New Orleans, and the nearby southwestern Louisiana parishes, "gumbo weather" is not a cutesy term. It's an actual season, beginning sometime in November when the temperature finally starts to drop and continuing at least through the Super Bowl, a huge gumbo day. (When I found an enormous pearl from an oyster in a seafood gumbo I'd made for Super Bowl XLIV, we put it on top of the TV as a talisman. I'm still convinced that's why the Saints won for the first time ever.) There are "gumbo weather" cookbooks and blogs; there's even a folk/blues band by the name somewhere in Texas. But for most of us, the words denote that joyous period when you can open the doors and windows to a cool breeze, put a pot on the stove, and maybe even wear a sweater.

The great characteristic of gumbo is that it's an infinitely flexible culinary art form—there are as many versions as there are people who make them. Cajun gumbos feature a roux so dark it all but hides the seemingly mysterious ingredients, giving rise to the all-too-common newspaper description of Louisiana politics as "a roiling gumbo of corruption." New Orleans Chef Donald Link makes a roux

Soundtrack for the cook: *Jimmy Buffett,* "I Will Play for Gumbo"

using 4 cups of flour and 3 cups of oil as a base for the seafood gumbo in his James Beard–award-winning *Real Cajun.* Most Creole versions, by contrast, are far lighter, with a base of no more than a couple of tablespoons of oil and flour, and often include tomatoes and okra.

The dish, named either for the Bantu word for okra *(kingombo)* or the Choctaw word for filé (*kombo,* the powder made from dried sassafras leaves that often serves as a thickener) originated in the eighteenth century, and is said to have been inspired by everything from French bouillabaisse to West African stews. Whatever, it's now its own delicious thing, rightly described as "an original conception" in *The Picayune Creole Cookbook* from 1901, which also refers to the "occult science of making a good 'Gombo à la Creole.'" Actually, it's not that hard. A dark roux requires more patience than skill, but the version I include here, with tomatoes, okra, and the de rigueur "holy trinity" of chopped onion, bell pepper, and celery, takes little time.

Ramos Gin Fizz

The Ramos Gin Fizz, one of the city's most iconic—and refreshing—cocktails, was invented by Henry Ramos in 1888. By 1915, the drink was so popular, Ramos had to hire dozens of "shaker boys" during Carnival season to meet the demand at his bar, the Imperial Cabinet Saloon—the trick to the cocktail's frothy outcome is the vigorous shake. Unlike most of his neighbors, Ramos closed his saloon at the onset of Prohibition. Once the Eighteenth Amendment was repealed, he sold his secret recipe to the Roosevelt Hotel. Huey Long, who kept a suite at the Roosevelt when he was governor, grew so partial to the drink that he took a hotel bartender with him on a trip to Manhattan. I don't blame him. A properly made gin fizz is an addictive tonic on a hot day and a hangover cure of some renown. Just don't forget to shake.

2 ounces (¼ cup) gin

1 ounce (2 tablespoons) simple syrup

½ ounce (1 tablespoon) freshly squeezed lemon juice

½ ounce (1 tablespoon) freshly squeezed lime juice

1 egg white

1 ounce (2 tablespoons) heavy cream

4 drops orange flower water

Chilled club soda

Combine the first seven ingredients in a cocktail shaker with ice. Shake vigorously.

Strain into a highball glass and top with club soda.

Cheese Thumbprint Wafers with Hot Pepper Jelly

Makes about 20 wafers

There is almost no combination of sharp cheese and flour and butter that I don't like, especially as an hors d'oeuvre with a cocktail. This particular cheese wafer is enlivened with a dab of pepper jelly and is a cinch to make.

Place the flour and salt in the bowl of a food processor fitted with a metal blade and pulse briefly to blend. Add the butter and pulse until the mixture has the texture of coarse cornmeal. Add the cheeses and blend until the dough begins to form a ball.

Transfer the dough to a lightly floured surface and gather it into a ball. Wrap the dough in plastic wrap and refrigerate for at least 30 minutes or up to two days.

Preheat the oven to 400°F. Line two baking sheets with parchment paper and set aside.

Shape the dough into 1-inch balls, using a scant tablespoon of dough for each one, and place 1 inch apart on the baking sheets. Bake for 5 minutes.

Remove from the oven and press your thumb into the top of each ball to create an indentation. Place about ½ teaspoon of jelly into each indentation and return the sheet to the oven. Bake until lightly browned, 6 to 8 more minutes.

1 cup all-purpose flour

¼ teaspoon salt

6 tablespoons butter, cut into ¼-inch pieces

1 ½ cups grated sharp cheddar cheese

½ cup grated Parmesan

½ cup hot pepper jelly, red or green

Seafood Gumbo

3 pounds medium shrimp

2 ½ teaspoons salt, plus a
generous pinch

¼ cup plus 2 tablespoons
vegetable oil

2 pounds okra, sliced

1 pound andouille sausage,
thinly sliced

2 tablespoons all-purpose flour

2 cups finely chopped
yellow onion

1 cup finely chopped celery

1 cup finely chopped
green bell pepper

1 cup chopped scallions, with
tender green parts

4 cloves garlic, minced

2 tablespoons tomato paste

3 bay leaves

1 teaspoon dried thyme

1 teaspoon Tabasco sauce

¼ teaspoon cayenne pepper

½ teaspoon freshly ground
black pepper

1 tablespoon Lea & Perrins
Worcestershire sauce

One 16-ounce can whole tomatoes, drained and roughly
chopped, liquid reserved

1 pound lump crabmeat

1 pint (2 to 3 dozen) oysters

¼ cup finely chopped Italian
parsley

Cooked white rice

I've been making this gumbo ever since I was in college and found a similar version in a Junior League cookbook, the name of which now escapes me. When I lived in New York in the 1980s and '90s, I served it along with a bucket of Popeyes fried chicken to my Yankee friends, who found both things wildly exotic. The okra added in the beginning gives the soup body, while the okra at the end provides texture. The all-important addition of andouille lends a deep flavor to the broth. If you can't find andouille, Polish sausage will do.

Remove the shrimp shells and heads. Cover and refrigerate the shrimp and place the shells and heads in a large pot. Add 8 cups water and a generous pinch of salt and bring the mixture to a boil over high heat. Reduce heat to medium low and simmer, partially covered, for 1 hour.

Cool slightly, then strain the seafood stock through a fine-mesh strainer. Discard the heads and shells and reserve the stock. (You may skip the latter part of this step and substitute 6 to 7 cups store-bought seafood stock. Either way, you must remove the shrimp shells and heads from the raw shrimp.)

In a large heavy skillet, heat 2 tablespoons of the oil over medium heat and add the okra (if using frozen okra, take it out of the freezer about 15 minutes ahead of time). Sprinkle with ½ teaspoon salt and sauté, stirring often, for 10 minutes.

Reserve the okra, wipe out the skillet, heat another tablespoon of oil over medium-high heat, and sauté the andouille until browned, about 8 minutes. Set aside.

In a large heavy pot, heat the remaining 3 tablespoons of oil over high heat. Add the flour, lower heat to medium, and stir constantly until the roux is a medium brown. Add the yellow onion, celery, and bell pepper, and sauté, stirring often, until the vegetables begin to soften, 4 to 5 minutes. Add ½ cup of the scallions and the garlic and cook for 3 more minutes. Stir in the tomato paste, bay leaves, thyme, Tabasco, cayenne, black pepper, Worcestershire sauce, and 2 tea-

1 cup all-purpose flour

¼ teaspoon salt

3 tablespoons butter,
    cut into ¼-inch chunks

2 tablespoons lard, cut into
    small chunks (vegetable
    shortening or more butter
    may be substituted)

About ¼ cup ice water

PARTIALLY BAKED PIE SHELL

Place the flour and salt in a food processor fitted with a steel blade. Pulse a few times to sift, then add the butter and lard. Pulse again until mixture looks like coarse cornmeal. Add 2 tablespoons of ice water. Pulse and add more water until the mixture just begins holding together but is not sticky or wet. Quickly gather it into a ball, lightly dust with flour, wrap well with plastic wrap, and flatten into a disk about a ½ inch thick with the heel of your hand. Refrigerate for at least 30 minutes and up to 2 days.

Preheat the oven to 375°F. Roll out the dough on a lightly floured surface until you have a circle roughly 13 ½ inches in diameter. Gently fold in half and then in half again. Place the folded pastry's point in the center of the pie plate, carefully unfold, and gently press into the edges of the plate. Trim (and save) any messy excess and crimp the edge decoratively.

Lightly butter a piece of foil, and drape it over the pie plate, buttered side down, so that it covers the edges. Press it very lightly into the contours of the pie shell. Fill with pie weights or dried beans.

Bake for 15 minutes, then remove the shell from the oven and carefully lift out the foil and beans. Prick the bottom with a fork and repair any cracks with reserved dough trimmings. Return the shell to the oven and bake until it begins to color and the bottom looks dry, about 10 more minutes.

GUMBO LOVE

My learned friend Jessica Harris (addressed properly as Dr. Jessica B. Harris) has been named a southern Louisiana food icon by the John Folse Culinary Institute and called the Maya Angelou of the culinary world. Certainly there is poetry in her writings about food, and she knows more about the cuisine of the African diaspora than anyone out there. Her books include *Beyond Gumbo: Creole Fusion Food from the Atlantic Rim, High on the Hog: A Culinary Journey from Africa to America,* and the deeply affecting *My Soul Looks Back: A Memoir.* Jessica was born and raised in New York, taught for years at Queens College, and has a summer place on Martha's Vineyard. But she also owns a charming cottage in the Marigny district of New Orleans, which she claims as home. Here, she explains her Southern roots and her late-in-life love of gumbo.

"I am profoundly a Southerner, but a Southerner who was born in the geographically displaced South, the result of the African-American Great Migration. My father was from a small town near Nashville; my maternal grandma was from Virginia and my paternal one was from Tennessee. So I can 'yes ma'am' with the best of them. I grew up with church hats, biscuits, and Alaga syrup—my father would swoon when he got his hands on sorghum and okra.

"Okra was contentious in my house as my mother was not fond of its mucilaginous properties, and I remember that it was the only vegetable I did not have to eat as a child. But eat it I did, and I loved it, much to my mother's amazement. As an adult, I reclaimed my love for okra on trips to the African continent, where I rediscovered it in multiple soupy stews that I learned were gumbo ancestors. When I had my first taste of Duck and Andouille Gumbo (see page 81) in New Orleans, I knew I'd hit my Nirvana. I have a shellfish allergy and so many of the gumbos of my adopted city are verboten. But the thick, dark, roux-rich liquid with pieces of savory duck and the peppery bite of andouille punctuated with my favorite pod have kept me from regretting that allergy for one instant. Truly, the mahogany-colored gumbo is food for the gods.

"That, though, is not my only gumbo. For the past decade or so, I've hosted a party each Holy Thursday for an increasing number of friends at Dooky Chase's Restaurant, where Leah Chase, the doyenne of Black Creole cooking in New Orleans, prepares her famous gumbo z'herbes. It is a verdant, meat-rich stew prepared for the last day on which meat can be eaten before Easter. Traditionally, there are an odd number of purchased or foraged greens that appear in the soup. The story goes that you will make a new friend for each type of green in the pot. Each year I host up to fifty people, and Mrs. Chase jokes that, unlike the other diners who eat and depart, I was among the first to hold a *boozin'* (her Creole term for an all-afternoon shindig)."

When Jessica craves duck and andouille gumbo, she heads uptown to Upperline or to Herbsaint, in the Warehouse District. Herbsaint chef/owner Donald Link's superlative recipe on the following spread.

DUCK AND ANDOUILLE GUMBO

Cut the duck into 8 to 10 pieces, leaving the bones in. Season with 2 teaspoons salt and 1 teaspoon black pepper and toss with ½ cup flour to coat. In a large sauté pan over high heat, heat the oil. Panfry the duck pieces until lightly golden and set aside. In the same oil, add the remaining 1 ½ cups flour and stir over medium heat for about 45 minutes until the roux reaches a nice dark-brown color. Add the chopped vegetables and the seasonings, including the remaining 1 tablespoon salt and 1 ½ teaspoons black pepper. Stir to combine.

Add 3 quarts chicken stock and the panfried duck pieces and bring to a boil. Be sure to stir occasionally so that the roux does not stick to the bottom. As soon as the mixture comes to a boil, set it at a low simmer. Simmer, skimming the fat from the top occasionally, until the duck is cooked through, 45 minutes to 1 hour. Add the andouille and simmer for another 30 to 45 minutes or until the duck meat begins to fall off the bone. If the gumbo still tastes of roux, add another 1 to 2 cups of stock. If you like okra in your gumbo, now would be the time to add it. Make sure you sauté it in vegetable oil first to get some of the sliminess out of it.

To serve, divide among individual soup bowls. Add a spoonful of rice to each serving, and top with sliced scallions.

One 4 ½-pound duck

1 tablespoon plus 2 teaspoons
  salt

2 ½ teaspoons freshly ground
  black pepper

2 cups all-purpose flour

1 ¼ cups vegetable oil

1 medium yellow onion,
  finely chopped

3 ribs celery, finely chopped

1 poblano pepper,
  finely chopped

1 green bell pepper,
  finely chopped

1 jalapeño pepper,
  finely chopped

3 cloves garlic, minced

1 teaspoon cayenne pepper

1 ½ teaspoons chili powder

1 teaspoon white pepper

1 teaspoon paprika

1 ½ teaspoons filé powder

3 quarts salted chicken stock,
  plus more as needed

1 pound andouille sausage,
  sliced into ½-inch-thick
  half-moons

2 cups sliced sautéed okra
  (optional)

Scant ¾ cup cooked white rice

1 bunch scallions, sliced, for
  garnish

MENU

ORANGE RUM GIMLET

TAPENADE

GRAND AIOLI

SATSUMA CAKE
with Mascarpone Cream

PETER PATOUT'S
FAMOUS
SATSUMACELLO

Aioli Dinner

Soundtrack for the cook: *Zachary Richard,* "Jolie Blonde," and *Mary Chapin Carpenter,* "Down at the Twist and Shout"

My friend Peter Patout's family has been farming and milling sugar since 1832. Located in Patoutville (where else?), M. A. Patout & Son is the oldest family owned and operated manufacturer of raw sugar and molasses in the United States. Peter, whose primary home is in New Orleans on Bourbon Street (see the Gumbo Lunch chapter), also keeps a place near the mill, a 1920s house that once belonged to his grandparents. When he's in residence there, I love to make the two-and-a-half-hour trek to what we call "Cajun country," the twenty-two-parish area that's home to the state's large Francophone population. Peter's ancestor Simeon Patout, for example, came over with his wife and children from Moliens, France.

There's no bad time to visit, but it is especially beautiful in summer and early fall, when the sugarcane is waist-high in the fields. In late fall and winter, the trucks full of cut cane form miles-long lines at the mill and there's twenty-four-hours-a-day drama as great clouds of smoke fill the sky. No matter what time of year I go, I fill up my cooler with Cajun meats and chaurice sausage at Poche's in Breaux Bridge or Hebert's in Maurice; we dine on crawfish bisque at the Yellow

Bowl in Jeanerette. And we always find time to drink and dance at least one night away at Peg's in Lydia.

As it happens, the artist George Rodrigue grew up just down the road in New Iberia, a lovely town on the Bayou Teche. When he died in 2013, he was most famous for his Blue Dog portraits featuring his own late dog Tiffany and based on the Cajun legend of the *loup garou,* or ghost dog. But when he began his career, he was most interested in documenting Cajun culture in works like *Aioli Dinner* (1971). This painting was based on the old Creole gourmet societies, which had their heyday between 1890 and 1920, when they met each month on the lawn of a different plantation house in and around New Iberia. I doubt a grand aioli was served on every occasion, but I love Rodrigue's image of the group, dressed in black and white, sharing a meal prepared by the women and served by the young boys.

A grand aioli is not often served in the Cajun parishes these days, which is a shame. A gorgeous-looking warm-weather feast that is a virtual symbol of French Provençal cuisine, it is not only celebratory but also easy and extravagant. It's all about the freshest ingredients perfectly prepared and accompanied by a garlicky mayonnaise

for dipping. Since pretty much everything is meant to be eaten with your hands, the platter encourages intimacy and camaraderie around the table—but at this particular meal, we were all good friends in the first place. Among the guests were Stephen Stirling, a gifted wood-carver (I can't live without his muddler or his rice spoon) who lives in nearby Franklin, and Angèle Parlange, whose family owns Parlange on the False River, the state's prettiest plantation house and the oldest one still in the hands of the original family.

In France, mussels and cod are the usual seafood; here, I put Louisiana's generous bounty of shrimp and crab and redfish to use on our platter. Everything is served at room temperature, making the spread even easier on the cook, and multiple cold bottles of rosé are required. For both cocktails and dessert, I made use of satsuma oranges, a type of mandarin plentiful in South Louisiana and one that grows all around Peter's property. Every year during the season, he brings me enormous baskets of the sweet, juicy fruit, and each Christmas, I look forward to a couple of bottles of his legendary homemade satsumacello.

Two more of Rodrigue's frequent subjects are Evangeline, the heroine of Henry Wadsworth Longfellow's epic poem who follows the path that many Cajuns took from Nova Scotia to Louisiana, and the *jolie blonde,* the character featured in a popular Cajun waltz. I think the artist would have approved of our gathering under the live oaks. He so respected the traditions of his ancestors, and Peter, with his antiques-filled houses and love of the land, honors the past and his own Louisiana history with more joie de vivre and élan than anyone I know.

Orange Rum Gimlet

Serves 1

Orange-infused rum is super easy to make and I use it in all sorts of cocktails. After you strain the rum, it will keep indefinitely. On occasions like the one here, you might not want to spend all your time shaking individual cocktails. You can make the drink in larger quantities by multiplying the ingredients by the number of servings you want. Stir everything up in a big pitcher and add ice and 1 or 2 sliced oranges or satsumas. You also can adjust the simple syrup to taste. Sticklers will say it's no longer technically a gimlet, but it's still delicious.

Slice the oranges or satsumas (if using oranges, cut the slices in half again) and place in a pitcher or a pot large enough to hold both the slices and the rum. Pour in the rum, cover, and let stand overnight. Strain.

Pour the rum, lime juice, Cointreau, and simple syrup into a cocktail shaker filled with ice. Shake and pour into a small glass. Cut the orange or satsuma slice in half and add as a garnish.

FOR THE RUM

2 large navel oranges or 4 or 5 satsumas
1 bottle (750 ml) white rum

FOR THE COCKTAIL

4 ounces strained rum
2 ounces freshly-squeezed lime juice
1 ounce Cointreau (you may also use Grand Marnier or triple sec, but I much prefer Cointreau)
1 ounce simple syrup
1 orange or satsuma slice for garnish

Tapenade

Makes about 1 ½ cups

Tapenade is one of the quickest, easiest things in the world to make, and I don't think I've ever found a version I didn't like. Some call for green olives, some include oil-packed tuna, some add roasted red peppers or eggplant. This recipe was inspired by one in Simone Beck's final cookbook and it taps into the menu's Provençal vibe and citrus theme. Sometimes I make like Simone and add a tablespoon of cognac, which is never a bad thing.

Place all the ingredients, except the olive oil, in the bowl of a food processor. Pulse to blend to a coarse puree. Add the olive oil and process only until the mixture is cohesive, but still a fairly coarse paste.

½ pound large Greek-style black olives, pitted and drained
6 anchovies in oil
2 tablespoons capers, drained
1 peeled clove garlic
2 teaspoons fresh thyme leaves
2 teaspoons orange zest
½ teaspoon whole fennel seed
⅛ teaspoon cayenne
4 tablespoons olive oil
Sliced baguette for serving

Grand Aioli

1 bag Zatarain's Crawfish,
    Shrimp, and Crab Boil

¼ cup plus 2 tablespoons salt

2 lemons, quartered

2 pounds shrimp, 16 to 20 count
    per pound, unpeeled

2 pounds fillets of redfish or any
    other firm white Gulf fish,
    such as grouper or cobia

16 to 20 new or fingerling
    potatoes, peeled

1 ½ pounds green beans or
    haricots verts, trimmed

6 large eggs

1 pound cooked blue crab claws

1 bunch radishes

I feel like some of the ingredients included here are non-negotiable (the shrimp, fish, potatoes, and green beans, for sure). On the other hand, you should feel free to use the recipe as a template of sorts. When I spot okra in the market (especially young pods), I steam it until it's tender but still a little crisp and add it to the platter. Ditto for baby zucchini, lightly steamed and halved. Yellow and/or red cherry tomatoes add some yummy color. Wedges of trimmed raw fennel bulbs and/or stalks of celery (preferably the tender yellow stalks with leaves still attached) provide a welcome bit of crunch. I always make 1 cup of each of the aioli versions below. If you plan to serve only one type of aioli (and the basic version is pretty perfect on its own), you should make a double or triple batch to be sure you don't run low.

Combine roughly 2 quarts of water, crab boil, 2 tablespoons salt, and lemons in a large stockpot or Dutch oven and bring to a boil over high heat. Reduce the heat and simmer for 5 minutes. Turn the heat back to high and add the shrimp. Cook, uncovered, for 3 minutes. (After about 2 minutes, pluck a shrimp from the water, run it under cold water and taste. You only want to cook them until they are no longer transparent in the center, but only just. My pet peeve is even one slightly overcooked shrimp.) Drain the shrimp in a colander, discarding the seasoning bag and lemon pieces.

As soon as the shrimp are cool enough to handle, peel them, leaving the tail pieces intact. Place in a large bowl, cover, and refrigerate until ready to use.

Fill the same large pot about halfway with water and 2 tablespoons salt, and bring to a boil over high heat. Reduce heat to simmer and slide in the fish fillets. Cook the fillets until just cooked through, about 6 minutes, depending on their size. (I use the James Beard principle of 10 minutes per inch of fish measured at the thickest point.) Remove the fish with a slotted spatula and transfer to a large plate or rimmed baking dish and blot with paper towels. Cover

and refrigerate until ready to use. Before serving, I usually pull the fish apart into large chunks.

Empty the pot, add another 2 quarts of water and 2 tablespoons salt. Bring to a boil. Lower the heat to a fairly strong simmer and add the potatoes. Cook until fork-tender, about 12 minutes. Remove the potatoes with a slotted spoon and while the water continues to simmer, place them on a rimmed sheet pan lined with a clean kitchen towel to cool.

Add the green beans or haricots verts to the simmering water and cook until tender, about 5 minutes. (If you are using skinny haricots verts, check them after 2 to 3 minutes.) Remove to another towel–lined sheet pan to cool.

Return the simmering water to a boil and lower the eggs into the pot using a slotted spoon. Cook for 10 minutes. Remove the eggs from the water and peel them quickly under cool running tap water. Cut in half lengthwise and set aside. Discard water.

Drain the crab claws, blot them dry, and remove any stray bits of shell.

Trim and wash the radishes and allow them to dry. Depending on their size, you may halve or quarter them or keep them whole.

Arrange all the ingredients in groups on one or two platters. Serve, family style, with the aioli for dipping.

BASIC AIOLI

Drape a kitchen towel over a small saucepan and set a small bowl over it. (This will hold the bowl in place.) Mash garlic and salt together with a spoon. Whisk in the egg yolks and 2 teaspoons of warm water. Whisking constantly, slowly drizzle in the plain olive oil, 1 teaspoon at a time, until the sauce is thickened and emulsified. Whisking constantly, add the extra-virgin olive oil in a slow, steady stream. If the mixture gets too stiff, add more water as needed. Stir in the pepper and lemon juice (You don't need a lot—I never use more than a teaspoon), and add more salt if needed.

LIME SRIRACHA AIOLI

Omit the lemon juice and black pepper at the end of the basic recipe, and instead stir in 2 teaspoons each of lime juice and sriracha. Feel free to increase or decrease the sriracha according to your preferences for heat.

SAFFRON AIOLI

Mix 2 teaspoons of warm water with ½ teaspoon of crumbled saffron threads. Substitute this mixture for the plain warm water at the beginning of the original recipe. Omit lemon juice and black pepper at the end, and season with a generous pinch of Espelette pepper.

Makes 1 cup

3 cloves garlic, peeled and
    finely grated
¼ teaspoon kosher salt,
    plus more to taste
2 large egg yolks,
    at room temperature
½ cup olive oil
½ cup extra-virgin olive oil
Freshly ground black pepper
    to taste
Freshly squeezed lemon juice
    to taste

NOTE: Classic aioli recipes call for mashing the salt and garlic in a mortar using a pestle, but one of my favorite chefs, Suzanne Goin (of Lucques, A.O.C., and Larder fame in Los Angeles), suggests the grater alternative, and it works brilliantly. Also, you can make the aioli in a blender or food processor, but I find the texture of the handmade version far preferable, and I swear it goes just as quickly.

Satsuma Cake with Mascarpone Cream

Satsumas, or any other thin-skinned oranges such as clementines or mandarins, are the perfect choice for this cake, which was inspired by a similar version by the uber-talented North Carolina–based chef Andrea Reusing (Lantern, The Durham). After the citrus slices are simmered for a few minutes in syrup, their skins are plenty tender enough to cut with a fork. I most often serve this cake as a dessert, but it's also great for breakfast or at teatime. Here, I accompany each slice with mascarpone cream (which is so addictive it's hard not to eat it on its own, with a spoon) and put bottles of Satsumacello (see recipe on page 99) and Charboneau Golden Rum (made in Natchez from sugarcane grown in fields near where our dinner was held) on the table for diners to help themselves to.

Finely grate the zest of two of the oranges and reserve for the cake batter. Halve the oranges and juice them. Strain the juice and reserve ⅓ cup.

Slice the remaining oranges into thin rounds no more than ¼ inch thick. Remove and discard any seeds. You will have more slices than you need, but this way you'll have your pick of the perfect ones.

Gently combine the orange juice, lemon juice, 1 cup sugar, ¼ teaspoon salt, and orange slices in a medium saucepan over low heat and bring to a slow simmer. Simmer gently until the peels are tender and the slices are soft and translucent but not falling apart, 6 to 7 minutes. Using a slotted spoon, carefully transfer the orange slices to a plate. Continue to simmer the syrup until it has reduced to ½ cup, about 10 minutes.

Preheat the oven to 375°F. Butter a 9- or 10-inch springform cake pan.

Place the butter and remaining ¾ cup sugar in the bowl of an electric mixer and beat at medium speed until fluffy. With the mixer still running, add the eggs and beat until well incorporated. Add the reserved orange zest and the vanilla and mix until combined.

8 small thin-skinned satsumas, clementines, mandarins, blood oranges, or small navel oranges

Juice of ½ lemon

1 ¾ cup sugar

½ teaspoon salt

8 tablespoons (1 stick) butter, at room temperature, plus more for greasing the pan

2 large eggs, at room temperature

1 ½ teaspoons pure vanilla extract

⅓ cup semolina flour

⅔ cup all-purpose flour

1 teaspoon baking powder

Mascarpone Cream (recipe follows), as an accompaniment

Whisk the semolina flour, all-purpose flour, baking powder, and the remaining ¼ teaspoon salt together in a small bowl. Add the mixture, a little at a time, to the batter and mix until it is just incorporated and no white streaks remain. The batter will be fairly thick. Pour or spoon it into the buttered cake pan and smooth the surface. Arrange the glazed citrus slices in a single layer on top of the cake. Discard (or eat) extra citrus slices and reserve the syrup.

Bake the cake for 15 minutes. Reduce the oven temperature to 350°F and bake 35 to 40 minutes more, for a total of 50 to 55 minutes, until the cake is an even golden brown and a toothpick inserted into the center comes out clean. Let the cake cool in the pan on a wire rack until warm, not hot. Using a wooden skewer, poke holes all over the surface of the cake. Brush the remaining glaze over the top using a pastry brush. Allow the cake to cool to room temperature on the rack before removing it from the pan.

MASCARPONE CREAM

Whisk together the mascarpone cheese, sugar, vanilla, and rum in a large bowl until just blended. Beat the heavy cream at medium speed with an electric mixer until fairly stiff peaks form. Fold the whipped cream into the mascarpone mixture. Cover and refrigerate until ready to serve.

Makes about 3 cups

**FOR THE
MASCARPONE CREAM**

1 cup mascarpone cheese

¼ cup confectioners' sugar

2 teaspoons pure vanilla extract

*2 teaspoons Charboneau
Golden Rum or a good dark
rum like Barbancourt*

1 cup heavy cream

There's no bad time to visit
Patoutville, but it is especially beautiful
in summer and early fall, when the
sugarcane is waist-high in the fields.
In late fall and winter, the trucks full of
cut cane form miles-long lines at the mill
and there's twenty-four-hours-a-day drama
as great clouds of smoke fill the sky.

Peter Patout's Famous Satsumacello

n the occasions that I've been lucky enough to spend time on Italy's Amalfi Coast, I think I've drunk at least half my weight in limoncello, which I adore. One Christmas a few years ago, my beloved friend Peter Patout gave me a bottle of his homemade satsumacello and I decided I love it even more. Served cold, it is delicious on its own and the perfect accompaniment to the Satsuma Cake with Mascarpone Cream on pages 95-96.

10 to 12 satsumas
1 bottle (750 ml) Everclear
3 cups sugar
2 cups water

Wash the satsumas in hot water with a vegetable brush to remove any residue of pesticide or wax. Pat them dry.

Carefully zest the satsumas with a zester or vegetable peeler, being careful not to include any white pith from the peel. (The pith, the white part underneath the rind, is too bitter and will spoil your satsumacello.)

Place the zest in a large jar and fill with the Everclear. Let sit at room temperature for at least ten days and up to forty days in a cool, dark place. Turn the jar upside down two or three times to help bring out the flavor of the zest. The zest will eventually turn white.

When ready to proceed, combine the sugar and water in a large saucepan. Bring to a boil and cook for about 5 minutes, until sugar is well dissolved.

Strain the Everclear/zest mixture through a fine mesh sieve lined with cheesecloth or a paper towel into the simple syrup mixture. Stir and allow to cool. When the satsumacello has cooled completely, you may pour it into individual bottles.

MENU

FRENCH 75

TARTLETS OF OYSTERS
in Fennel Cream

**BIENVILLE
STUFFED MUSHROOMS**

**GEORGES PERRIER'S
CRAB CAKES**
with Meaux Mustard Beurre Blanc

**SMOKY ROASTED ROHAN
DUCK GOODENOUGH**
with Sauce "l'Orange"

**JASON'S MOM'S
"CHRISTMAS POTATOES"**

BRAISED RED CABBAGE
with Bacon & Riesling

BETH'S BANANA TARTE TATIN
*with Brown Sugar Rum
Ice Cream*

reveillon

Soundtrack for the cook: *Louis Armstrong,* "Christmas in New Orleans;" *The Subdudes,* "Peace in the World;" and *Allen Toussaint,* "Silent Night, Holy Night"

The word *reveillon,* translated from the French, means awakening or arousal. In nineteenth-century New Orleans, then, reveillon repasts were aptly named since they were served well after midnight. On Christmas Eve, the predominantly Catholic population would return home from midnight mass famished, and sit down to an especially generous multi-course spread that included breakfast dishes and breads, but also turtle soup, oysters, grillades of veal, and some sort of game, along with a vast array of sweets and wines and cordials. In France, the reveillon meal was particularly luxurious, featuring such items as lobster, oysters, and foie gras, along with a traditional turkey with chestnuts, followed by a *bûche de noël.* In both cases, the feast would last well into the early morning, often until dawn.

The New Orleans tradition had all but died out by the

1940s, but some fifty years ago, the idea, at least, was revived by the city's restaurateurs, who now offer reveillon menus throughout the holiday season. I prefer the at-home version, and since my own Christmas Eve church service is over by the early evening, dinner guests can be home—maybe—by midnight. Here, I combine the excess of both the Creole and the French menus, showcasing game and seafood and tapping into a handful of New Orleans traditions.

To help me design and prepare the feast, I called on my good friend the exceptionally gifted chef Jason Goodenough. Jason, who spent his childhood in Manhattan and London, graduated from the Culinary Institute of America and worked under one of my very favorite French chefs Georges Perrier, former chef/owner at the late, great Le Bec-Fin in Philadelphia. We have lots in common, including the fact that Jason's divine wife, Amelia, hails from the Mississippi Delta, where I grew up. In 2014 they settled in New Orleans with their two children, and Jason opened the critically acclaimed Carrollton Market, one of my more frequent stops in the city. No matter what Jason does with duck, it's always beyond delicious, so I knew he'd come up with something both traditional and innovative (check out his bacon blanket on the breasts) for our dinner. He also introduced me to his mother's miraculously easy side dish: a gratin of potatoes that I've now enthusiastically adopted.

For the dessert, I pressed Beth Biundo, another dear friend and frequent collaborator, into duty with a more elegant (and tasty) riff on New Orleans's much-revered bananas Foster. When we first met, Beth was creating serious magic as the pastry chef at yet another of my favorite restaurants Lilette. After a brief stint as an interior designer, she recently opened up Beth Biundo Sweets, and the city is far better for it.

The setting, the Italianate Garden District manse belonging to Sara and Paul Costello, more than matched the opulence of the menu. I'd known Sara and Paul in Manhattan, but after they made the move to New Orleans (settling barely four blocks from my own abode) in 2012, we became far

> *I combine the excess of both the Creole and the French menus, showcasing game and seafood and tapping into a handful of New Orleans traditions.*

faster friends. I adore their three children, and this book will now make the third that Paul and I have happily collaborated on. Since their gorgeous jewel box of a dining room is small (and most often home to a ping-pong table), we used it as a serving spot and instead seated guests at a long table set up for the night in their wide center hall. For the occasion, I brought over my great-grandmother's stemmed garnet glasses and her gilt-and-garnet-rimmed porcelain plates, a pile of silver, buckets of red roses, and most important, my long-time party assistants (and all-round life managers) Lisa Rogers and Terrell ("Cheaky") Johnson, whose grandmother helped me put on the first party I ever gave in New Orleans more than twenty years ago.

Sara and Paul and I tapped into the holiday spirit by inviting a handful of close friends and their kids (some of whom we pressed into duty as servers), and a good time was had by all. Though we didn't offer quite the same array of wines and cordials as the early Creoles, we served a lovely Puligny-Montrachet with the crab cakes and a Châteauneuf-du-Pape with the duck. With the dessert, there was aged rum and Cognac.

French 75

The French 75 cocktail is—aptly—named for a rapid-firing French field gun first put to use during World War I and was created around 1915 in Harry's New York Bar in Paris. The recipe in *The Savoy Cocktail Book,* which was published in 1930 and popularized the drink, calls for gin rather than Cognac and was the version I used until now. For this occasion, I decided to channel the New Orleans cocktail guru and super-nice guy Chris Hannah, who presided over Arnaud's French 75 Bar and who always uses Cognac. His take also adjusts the usual fifty/fifty measure of lemon juice and simple syrup for an overall drier drink.

Combine the first three ingredients in a mixing tin or shaker filled with ice and shake. Strain into a Champagne glass. Top with Champagne. Garnish with a lemon peel.

1 ¼ ounces (2 tablespoons plus 1 ½ teaspoons) Cognac

⅓ ounce (1 ¾ teaspoons) freshly squeezed lemon juice

¼ ounce (1 ½ teaspoons) simple syrup

2 ¼ ounces (¼ cup plus 1 ½ teaspoons) brut Champagne

Lemon peel

NOTE: When making this drink for a crowd, I multiply the first three ingredients by the number of cocktails I want to make and mix them together in the shaker with no ice. Keep the shaker in the refrigerator until ready to serve. Add ice, shake, and pour about 2 ⅓ ounces (scant ⅓ cup) of the mixture in the bottom of each flute. Fill the glasses with Champagne and garnish with lemon peel.

Tartlets of Oysters in Fennel Cream

Makes 24 tartlets

1 large bulb fennel or 2 smaller bulbs, trimmed and thinly sliced

2 tablespoons olive oil

3 tablespoons butter

1 teaspoon salt, plus more to taste

¼ cup plus 1 tablespoon Pernod or Herbsaint

2 tablespoons finely chopped shallots

White pepper to taste

½ cup heavy cream

24 oysters

Tabasco sauce

24 Beth's Mini Pastry Shells (recipe follows)

Even though these tartlets are napped with a bit of cream, they are actually fairly light and delicately flavored (as well as supremely elegant). Oysters and fennel have a marvelous affinity for each other—fennel tops are among the ingredients in properly made oysters Rockefeller, for example. This particular pairing hearkens back to one of my favorite dishes at the late and much-lamented Peristyle, when my friend Anne Kearney was the amazing chef there. She did an appetizer of oysters in an Herbsaint- or Pernod-scented cream sauce that I must have eaten at least once a week. Hers was a bit richer (it had the always-welcome addition of bacon), but since I'm practically killing people with kindness via the many luxurious dishes on the menu, I thought I'd opt for the lighter bite. But it's still the holidays, after all, and no matter what, you have to have oysters.

Roughly chop the fennel slices into thin slivers, 1 to 1 ½ inches long. Heat the oil with 1 tablespoon of the butter in a medium skillet or sauté pan over medium heat. Add the fennel and cook, stirring occasionally, until soft, about 10 minutes. If the fennel begins to stick to the pan, add a bit of water. When the fennel is soft, season with salt and deglaze the pan with 1 tablespoon of Pernod or Herbsaint, stirring constantly for a few seconds until the liqueur has all but evaporated. Remove the pan from the heat, place the fennel in a small bowl, and set aside.

Add the remaining 2 tablespoons of butter to the pan (no need to wipe it out), and melt it over medium heat. Add the shallots and cook for about 2 minutes, stirring constantly, until they are soft. Add ½ teaspoon of salt and a pinch of pepper.

Remove the pan from the stove and add the remaining ¼ cup of Pernod or Herbsaint. Set the pan back on the burner and simmer for 1 minute. Whisk in the cream and cook for 2 minutes more. Add the oysters, the remaining ½ teaspoon salt, and another pinch of pepper. Cook until the edges of the oysters just begin to curl, 2 to 3 minutes. Remove the pan from heat.

til the cheese is melted and well incorporated. Remove the pan from heat and discard the bay leaf. Taste for seasoning.

Preheat the oven to 375°F. Pull the stems from the whole mushrooms and place on the caps a rimmed baking sheet. Spoon a generous amount of stuffing into each one and top with some of the bread crumbs. Bake until the mushrooms are cooked through and the bread crumbs are toasted, 20 to 25 minutes. Transfer to a platter and serve immediately.

NOTE: To make classic oysters Bienville, shuck 2 dozen plump oysters. (If you have your fishmonger do it for you, ask him/her to reserve the flatter half of each shell.) Wash the shells and pat them dry. Preheat the oven to 400°F, and place the oysters in their shells in a large roasting pan lined with ½ inch of rock salt. Spoon a generous tablespoon of the Bienville mixture over each oyster, and top with the prepared bread crumbs. Bake for 10 to 15 minutes until just browned and slightly bubbling. If serving as a first course, transfer anywhere from 3 to 6 baked oysters to each oyster plate (if you have oyster plates—otherwise salad plates will do) and garnish with lemon wedges. You may also arrange the oysters on a platter with small plates or napkins and lots of oyster forks in a glass alongside and offer them as an hors d'oeuvre.

Georges Perrier's Crab Cakes with Meaux Mustard Beurre Blanc

Serves 8 to 10

14 ounces large shrimp, peeled and deveined

1 bunch scallions, sliced into thin rings

3 tablespoons butter

2 large eggs, cold

2 cups heavy cream, icy cold

2 tablespoons Meaux (or Dijon) mustard

1 tablespoon Lea & Perrins Worcestershire sauce

1 tablespoon Tabasco sauce

1 pound jumbo lump crabmeat, picked clean

2 tablespoons olive oil

Since Jason and I both revere Georges Perrier, I decided to serve the master's crab cakes as a first course. But to call these ethereal creations 'crab cakes' is to do them a disservice. Rather than using the usual bread crumbs and/or mayonnaise as a binder, Perrier employs a stiff puree of uncooked shrimp and keeps the cakes together while cooking via metal ring molds. Jason serves a version of these at Carrollton Market with sauce maltaise (an orange-flavored hollandaise) on a bed of sautéed fennel (rather than the endive here) and they are delicious. For this occasion, I lend a traditional beurre blanc sauce a New Orleans touch by adding Creole mustard.

TO MAKE THE CRAB CAKES

Chill shrimp along with the bowl and metal blade of a food processor in the freezer for about 30 minutes.

Sauté the scallions in 1 tablespoon of butter until just wilted. Set aside to cool.

Place the shrimp in the processor and puree on high speed for 1 minute or until smooth and shiny. Using a rubber spatula, scrape down the sides of the bowl, then add the eggs. Process again until mixture is smooth and shiny, about 2 minutes. Scrape the bowl again. With the machine running, slowly pour in the cream. Scrape the bowl and process again to make sure the cream is completely incorporated. Remove the mixture and place in a mixing bowl. Stir in the mustard, Worcestershire, and Tabasco, then gently fold in the cooled scallions and the crabmeat.

Place as many oiled 3-inch ring molds as will fit comfortably in a lightly oiled nonstick pan. Fill each mold with the mixture, smoothing off the tops with a spoon. Over medium heat, cook the crab cakes until golden brown, about 2 minutes on each side.

Once the cakes have browned, push down on the ring molds to

cut off any excess crab mixture and remove the rings from around the crab cakes. Remove the cakes from pan. Repeat until all the crab mix has been cooked. (The cakes can be made up to one day ahead of time up to this point and refrigerated.)

**FOR THE
BEURRE BLANC**

*2 tablespoons plus 1 ½
teaspoons white wine
vinegar*

*2 tablespoons plus 1 ½
teaspoons freshly squeezed
lemon juice*

1 tablespoon minced shallot

½ teaspoon salt

⅛ teaspoon white pepper

*18 tablespoons (2 sticks plus 2
tablespoons) butter, chilled*

1 tablespoon Creole mustard

TO MAKE THE BEURRE BLANC

In a medium saucepan, bring the vinegar, lemon juice, shallot, salt, pepper, and 2 tablespoons butter to a boil over high heat. Cook until reduced to a syrupy consistency. 1 ½ to 2 tablespoons should remain.

Cut the remaining 2 sticks of butter into 16 pieces. Remove saucepan from heat and immediately beat in 2 pieces of the butter. As the butter melts into the liquid, beat in another piece. Place the saucepan back on very low heat and, beating constantly, add pieces of butter in succession, as each one has almost dissolved into the sauce. The mixture should be very thick and ivory colored. Remove from heat and beat or whisk in the mustard until fully incorporated. This is best served immediately, but if you need to hold it for a bit, place the saucepan over barely warm water.

FOR THE ENDIVE

1 tablespoon butter

*2 teaspoons freshly squeezed
lemon juice*

*3 heads Belgian endive, cored
and cut into 1-inch slices*

1 teaspoon sugar

Salt to taste

White pepper to taste

TO MAKE THE ENDIVE

In a small skillet or sauté pan, melt the butter and the lemon juice over medium heat. Add the endive slices and the sugar and toss together. Cook until the endive is wilted but not soft and the pan juices have been absorbed. Season to taste and set aside.

TO ASSEMBLE THE DISH

Preheat the oven to 400ºF. Place the crab cakes on a buttered nonstick baking sheet and bake for 5 minutes, until cakes are springy to the touch. Place a small mound of endive on each serving plate, top with one or two of the cakes, and ladle a small amount of sauce over each one. Serve immediately.

Smoky Roasted Rohan Duck Goodenough with Sauce "l'Orange"

Two 5- to 6-pound Rohan ducks or similar fresh birds
Kosher salt to taste
2 to 2 ½ pounds top-quality, thick-sliced bacon, such as Benton's or Nueske's

From Jason: "I love eating a whole roasted duck; however, I frequently am unhappy with the way it turns out. As a fine dining chef, I want the breasts to be cooked medium but the legs cooked through completely. This method helps to achieve that—the thick-cut bacon insulates the breasts while the legs have direct access to the heat. By the time the legs are cooked through, the breasts are a beautiful medium. But that's not the only benefit. While the bacon is cooking, it releases its fat, which cascades down the skin of the duck and coats it with flavor. The duck breasts are essentially basting themselves in amazing, top-quality, smoky bacon fat. Halfway through the cooking process, the bacon weave is removed. Chop it up, sprinkle with a little bit of brown sugar and a splash of bourbon, and throw it back in the oven for a few minutes and you have a beautiful bourbon-candied bacon snack while you wait on the duck to cook."

Remove the bags of organs from the ducks. Clip the wings from the ducks, taking as little flesh along with them as possible. Place the wings and the necks in a Ziploc bag and refrigerate. Discard the other organs.

Bring a very large stockpot of water to a hard simmer and add a generous pinch of salt. Lower the first duck into the water carefully, until it is completely covered. Simmer until the skin is blistered, about 5 minutes. Carefully remove the duck from the hot water and repeat the process with the second duck. Blot the ducks dry and place in a large roasting pan, uncovered, in the refrigerator overnight to air-dry.

When ready to cook the ducks, preheat the oven to 425°F. Cut the strips of bacon in half the long way. Weave bacon strips perpendicular to each other over the breasts of the ducks so that they form a single layer. Ensure that only the breasts are covered, and that they are covered in their entirety. Trim the bacon around the thighs and wings, but again, ensure that none of the breast is exposed.

Place the ducks in the oven and roast until the bacon weave crisps up and shrinks (it will become smaller than the area it's supposed to cover), 35 to 45 minutes. Open the oven and carefully remove the bacon from the birds. Do not be concerned that the skin looks raw; it will caramelize while the birds finish. Take advantage of the oven door being open and baste the birds with some of the fat that has collected in the bottom of the pan, carefully spooning it up and pouring it over them.

Continue roasting the ducks, basting them periodically. When the thickest part of each thigh registers 155°F, remove the ducks from the oven. (Check the ducks after about 1 hour—they may need to cook at least 10 to 15 minutes more, depending on their weight.) Carefully remove the ducks from the pan to a platter and allow them to rest at least 30 minutes, but ideally 1 hour. (Leave the oven on while the ducks rest.) This process will keep the juices from pouring out of the bird when you carve it. Personally, I prefer a juicy mouthful rather than a juice-covered plate.

Prior to serving, return the birds to the roasting pan. Warm in the oven for about 5 minutes. Pull the ducks out, carve them, sauce them, and feast.

SAUCE "L'ORANGE"

Heat a large, heavy-bottomed saucepan over medium high heat. Add vegetable oil—and let it get very hot. Add the reserved duck parts and cook them until they are well browned, turning to ensure all sides are evenly cooked. Remove from the pan and reserve. Add the vegetables. Cook, stirring occasionally, until caramelized, 5 to 8 minutes. Return the duck parts to the pan and add the tomato paste. Stir to coat the ingredients evenly, and continue stirring until the tomato paste lightens in color.

Add the liqueur. It may flame up—if it does, shake the pan constantly to ensure the top layer of ingredients doesn't burn. When the liquid has reduced by half, add the stock, thyme, rosemary, and peppercorns. Reduce heat to medium-low and allow liquid to reduce by at least half again. Strain through a fine mesh sieve, season with salt to taste, and serve alongside the duck.

Makes about 1 ¾ cups

3 tablespoons vegetable oil
Reserved duck neck and wings
1 small yellow onion, sliced
½ carrot, roughly chopped
2 ribs celery, thinly sliced
2 tablespoons tomato paste
3 cups Cointreau or Grand Marnier
1 quart dark duck stock or store-bought chicken stock
2 sprigs thyme
1-inch sprig fresh rosemary
1 teaspoon black peppercorns
Kosher salt to taste

Jason's Mom's "Christmas Potatoes"

One 5.2-ounce package
   Boursin cheese with garlic
   and fine herbs
2 cups heavy cream
3 pounds baking potatoes
Pinch of kosher salt
8 ounces Parmigiano
   Reggiano, grated

This is the dish Jason says his mom invariably makes for Christmas and special birthdays to accompany duck—but also roasted beef, veal, or pork. I will now add it to my own repertoire because it's completely genius—since the cheese is already well seasoned, you needn't do much of anything to the potatoes. As Jason says, "These potatoes are as simple as they appear, and are so delicious they could change your life for the better." I concur and so did our guests.

Place the Boursin and cream in a large saucepan or heavy-bottomed Dutch oven over medium-low heat, stirring frequently until the Boursin melts. Be careful not to scorch the cream. Remove from heat.

Peel the potatoes and slice thinly, 1/8 inch or less, using a mandoline or the slicer attachment on a food processor.

Preheat the oven to 375°F.

Fold the potatoes into the cream mixture. Return the pan to medium-low heat and cook, stirring mixture constantly, until the cream thickens. Add a generous pinch of salt—enough so that the cream mixture tastes pretty salty. The potatoes will absorb the seasoning.

Pour the mixture into a 9 by 13–inch baking dish and cover with the grated cheese. Bake for 1 hour or until the cheese is golden brown and potatoes are fork-tender.

Braised Red Cabbage with Bacon & Riesling

I discovered a version of this cabbage years ago in Paul Bertolli's indispensable *Chez Panisse Cooking*. I make it with red cabbage at Christmas for a burst of festive color and with green cabbage on New Year's Day (with black-eyed peas of course) to signify the greenbacks you hope will come pouring in during the rest of the year. Either way, it is an easy and delicious side dish that I promise you'll come back to again and again.

Slice the cabbages in half, remove the cores, and cut the cabbages into rough chunks about 1 inch wide.

Warm the oil in a large Dutch oven over medium heat. Add the carrots, celery, onion, bacon, thyme, and wine and bring to a simmer. Put half the cabbage in the pot and sprinkle with 2 teaspoons of the salt and some freshly ground pepper. Add the remaining cabbage and repeat with remaining salt and additional pepper.

Cover the pot tightly and braise the cabbage over low heat. After about 25 minutes, stir the cabbage gently so that the leaves on top move to the bottom and the vegetables and bacon are distributed throughout. Replace the cover and cook another 20 minutes, or until the cabbage is tender. Taste the cabbage and correct for salt and pepper. Add the vinegar and toss well. The cabbage can be made several hours in advance and warmed in the same pot just before serving.

2 heads red cabbage, about 2 pounds

¼ cup olive oil

2 carrots, peeled and chopped

1 large rib celery, finely chopped

1 large yellow onion, finely chopped

8 ounces smoked bacon, sliced ¼ inch thick, cut crosswise into 1-inch pieces (If you can't get slices that thick from your butcher, use thick-cut smoked bacon, such as Benton's or Nueske's.)

2 teaspoons fresh thyme leaves

1 ¼ cups slightly sweet Riesling or Gewürztraminer

1 tablespoon salt

Freshly ground black pepper to taste

2 tablespoons cider vinegar

Beth's Banana Tarte Tatin with Brown Sugar Rum Ice Cream

Serves 8

1 batch tart dough
(recipe follows)

4 bananas, sliced lengthwise

1 ½ cups sugar

½ cup water

2 tablespoons butter

½ teaspoon cinnamon

2 tablespoons dark rum

Ella Brennan invented bananas Foster in 1951 when she was at the helm of the legendary Brennan's restaurant in the French Quarter. It's a supremely easy dessert made by sautéeing sliced bananas in butter and brown sugar before flaming them with rum and serving them over vanilla ice cream. Ella herself said she vastly preferred crêpes suzette, but the warm banana dessert is still prepared tableside at Brennan's and has become a dish that is synonymous with the city. For a slightly more elegant take, I asked Beth, one of the most talented pastry chefs in the country, to invent her own bananas Foster tart, and she came up with this divine version accompanied by a scoop of brown sugar rum ice cream to cover all the bases.

Remove the dough from the refrigerator and, on a lightly floured surface, roll into a ½-inch-thick circle that is 11 to 12 inches in diameter. Return the rolled dough to the refrigerator.

Arrange the bananas in a pinwheel shape in the bottom of a 10-inch-round tart or cake pan. Preheat the oven to 375°F.

Combine the sugar and water in a small heavy-bottomed saucepan over high heat. Cook until the sugar begins to caramelize, then lower the heat and cook, stirring constantly, until the mixture is a warm caramel color. Remove from heat and stir in the butter, cinnamon, and rum. Pour the caramel evenly over the bananas.

Place the pan with the bananas on a rimmed baking sheet. Remove the rolled dough from the refrigerator and drape it over the bananas, tucking the edges down inside the pan. Bake until the dough is browned and cooked through, about 40 minutes.

Remove from oven and let the tart rest for 15 minutes. Invert a serving plate over the tart pan. Turn the plate and pan over together and carefully remove the pan. Slice into 8 pieces and serve with Brown Sugar Rum Ice Cream (recipe follows). Whipped cream or vanilla ice cream would be fine substitutes.

FOR THE TART DOUGH

16 tablespoons cold cream
cheese, cubed

16 tablespoons (2 sticks)
cold unsalted butter,
cut into cubes

1 ½ cups all-purpose flour

FOR THE ICE CREAM

2 cups heavy cream

1 cup whole milk

¾ cup firmly packed
brown sugar

5 large egg yolks, lightly beaten

2 tablespoons dark rum

1 teaspoon pure vanilla extract

TART DOUGH

Combine all ingredients in the bowl of a stand mixer fitted with the paddle attachment and beat until the dough just comes together. Gather up and form into a small disk and wrap snugly in plastic wrap. Refrigerate for at least 2 hours and up to 5 days.

BROWN SUGAR RUM ICE CREAM

Bring 1 cup of the cream (keep the other cup refrigerated), milk, and brown sugar to a boil in a heavy-bottomed saucepan over high heat. Lower heat and keep the mixture at a simmer.

Place the egg yolks in a medium mixing bowl and whisk half the hot cream mixture into the yolks. Pour the egg/cream mixture back into the pan and whisk to blend. Cook until mixture is just thickened and coats the back of a spoon Remove from heat and stir in the remaining 1 cup cold cream, rum, and vanilla. Strain through a fine mesh sieve and refrigerate for 30 minutes or overnight. Freeze in an ice-cream maker according to the manufacturer's instructions.

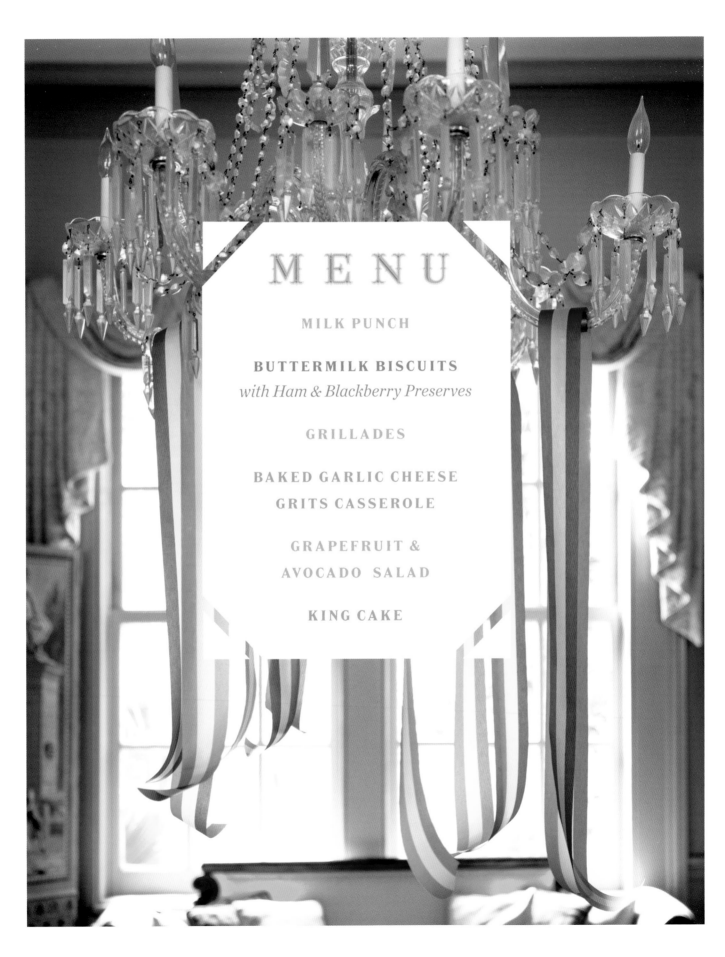

MENU

MILK PUNCH

BUTTERMILK BISCUITS
with Ham & Blackberry Preserves

GRILLADES

BAKED GARLIC CHEESE
GRITS CASSEROLE

GRAPEFRUIT &
AVOCADO SALAD

KING CAKE

Mardi Gras

Mardi Gras Brunch

In New Orleans, the Mardi Gras season—a city-wide bacchanalia that includes (but is by no means limited to) a string of public parades, private balls, and raucous street parties—officially kicks off on Twelfth Night and comes to a spectacular close on Shrove Tuesday, the day before Ash Wednesday. An inextricable part of the city's identity from its earliest days, Mardi Gras, also known as Carnival, now contributes more than $500 million to the city's economy.

In 1699, when French-Canadian explorer Jean-Baptiste Le Moyne, Sieur de Bienville arrived at a spot sixty miles downriver from where New Orleans is today, he named it Pointe de Mardi Gras—his men reminded him that they'd landed on the eve of the holiday. America's first Mardi Gras celebration was held in 1703 at the nearby Fort Louis de la Louisiane (now Mobile, Alabama), and when Bienville founded New Orleans in 1718, the settlers were eager to show up their neighbors. An 1835 account by James R. Creecy, a visitor to the city, provides vivid testimony to their success: "All of the *mischief* of the city is 'alive and wide awake'... Men and boys, women and girls, bond and free, white and black, yellow and brown, exert themselves to invent and appear in grotesque, quizzical, diabolical, horrible, humorous, strange masks and disguises. Human bodies are seen with heads of beasts and birds; beasts and birds with human heads." Further, Creecy wrote, all manner of maskers, in guises ranging from mermaids to monks, "parade and march on foot, on horseback, in wagons, carts, coaches . . . in rich confusion, up and down the streets, wildly shouting, singing, laughing, drumming, fiddling, fifing, and *all throwing flour broad-cast* as they wend their reckless way."

During the second half of the nineteenth century, when the Anglo-Americans had pretty much wrested economic and political power from the founding Creoles, those wild impromptu marches gave way to more organized official parades and balls, put on by private Carnival clubs or "krewes." In 1875 Mardi Gras was declared a legal state holiday, and it has been celebrated ever since, even (or especially) in the year following Hurricane Katrina, when it was deemed too crucial to the city's economic (and emotional) recovery not to take place.

During that cathartic Mardi Gras, the best of the parades featured enormous papier-mâché floats lampooning those who had failed the city most, from the U.S. Army Corps of Engineers (responsible for the failed levees) to the countless local and national politicians who had not exactly risen to the occasion. What visitors to the city saw during the Carnival of 2006 was what outsiders always see: overflowing bars, restaurants, and nightclubs; impromptu "second lines" (folks gyrating and parading behind marching bands); Mardi Gras Indians in their elaborately beaded costumes; masked float riders tossing "throws" ranging from beads and doubloons to "go cups" (a collection of festive plastic cups is a necessity in New Orleans since it is perfectly legal to consume alcohol on the streets—at any time of year—so long as it is not in a glass container).

I rode in a giant red shoe while thousands of people jumped up and down, frantically chanting my name.

What visitors generally don't see are the balls thrown by the old-line krewes, including Comus and Rex, in which the courts are made up of debutantes, one of whom reigns as queen, complete with an elaborately beaded gown and scepter (a queen's dress typically requires forty hours of beading; and there is such a thing as "scepter school"). The closest I'll ever come to being a queen—or a rock star for that matter—was my stint three years ago as honorary muse in the all-female Krewe of Muses parade. I rode in a giant red shoe while thousands of people jumped up and down, frantically chanting my name in hopes that I might toss them one of the season's most coveted prizes, a bejeweled shoe (second only to the Krewe of Zulu's glittered coconuts). It was a ton of fun and I'm forever grateful to the Muses, whose floats are among the city's most creative and satirical.

Usually, though, I am among the parade watchers and party givers. My favorite gathering to host is a brunch on the last Sunday before Mardi Gras, when so many of my pals are in need of a restorative but festive pick-me-up after nights (and days) on end of carousing. The menu is pretty much designed to cure a hangover (to this end, I also employ it during big wedding weekends and similar multi-day shindigs) and send the guests well fed and happily back out onto the streets

to parade watch, milk punch in hand. For dessert, I offer a variety of king cakes from my favorite purveyors. Tradition has it that the guest who gets the piece containing the bean or the baby (or the pig, if the cake comes from Cochon Butcher) must host the following year's event. This particular party was held at the Garden District house of my dear friends Melissa and John D. Gray, who have by far the loveliest dining room in town—and one that happens to be painted in a tasteful shade of Mardi Gras yellow.

When you're out and about during Mardi Gras, the streets themselves provide a constant soundtrack via marching bands and second lines, impromptu street gatherings, and music spilling out of bars and clubs. But if you're having a party and you don't have live music on hand, this playlist is a good place to start.

MARDI GRAS PLAYLIST

"GO TO THE MARDI GRAS"
Professor Longhair

"MARDI GRAS MAMBO"
The Hawkettes

"HEY POCKY A-WAY"
The Meters

"MARDI GRAS IN NEW ORLEANS"
Dirty Dozen Brass Band

"NIGHT PEOPLE"
Robert Palmer

"NEW SUIT"
The Wild Magnolias

"LET THE GOOD TIMES ROLL"
Dr. John

"SOCIAL AID AND PLEASURE CLUB"
The Subdudes

"BIG CHIEF"
Professor Longhair and Earl King

"WHEN THE SAINTS GO MARCHING IN"
Louis Armstrong

Milk Punch

I adore a properly made Bloody Mary and I would not turn down a refreshing screwdriver, but there is no better hangover cure on earth than a milk punch. Addictively tasty and immediately restorative, it is a staple in bars and restaurants that understand such things (Galatoire's offers up an especially good one, as does Commander's Palace), and de rigueur at daytime Mardi Gras gatherings.

Make a simple syrup by combining the sugar and water in a saucepan. Bring to a boil, cooking just until all the sugar has dissolved, 3 to 5 minutes. Allow the syrup to cool. It may be stored, refrigerated in a jar, for up to two weeks.

Whisk the milk and the cream together in a large pitcher or punch bowl until blended. Stir in the spirits and vanilla. Add ½ cup of the simple syrup. Taste and add more simple syrup as needed.

Refrigerate until thoroughly chilled. To serve, pour into highball glasses and grate nutmeg on top.

½ cup sugar

½ cup water

1 quart (4 cups) whole milk

1 pint (2 cups) heavy cream

2 cups brandy

1 cup bourbon

1 tablespoon pure vanilla extract

Freshly grated nutmeg for garnish

Buttermilk Biscuits with Ham & Blackberry Preserves

Makes about 24 small sandwiches

4 cups all-purpose flour

1 tablespoon plus 1 ½ teaspoons baking powder

1 tablespoon salt

1 teaspoon baking soda

20 tablespoons (2 ½ sticks) butter, frozen, cut into ½-inch cubes

1 cup buttermilk

12 thin slices smoked ham

4 tablespoons (½ stick) melted butter

One 12-ounce jar blackberry preserves or green pepper jelly

I've given enough Mardi Gras brunches to know that the first thing people crave after a night of revelry (other than some liquid refreshment, of course) is a salty, buttery treat, preferably one that is warm and bite-size. A ham biscuit is the perfect thing, particularly if you cut the biscuits an inch and a half in diameter. These biscuits are especially flaky thanks to the frozen butter and the last-minute refrigeration before baking. A smear of blackberry preserves provides a sweet counterpoint to the smoky ham—as well as a touch of Mardi Gras color. For a bit of heat, try green pepper jelly instead. You'll still be firmly in the Mardi Gras color range.

In a large mixing bowl, whisk together the flour, baking powder, salt, and baking soda to blend. Using a pastry blender or two knives, cut the butter into the flour mixture until the butter is the size of peas. (You can also do this with your fingers.) Add the buttermilk and mix with a wooden spoon until the dough comes together.

Turn the dough onto a lightly floured surface and sprinkle the top with flour. Gently flatten by pushing the dough away from you. Fold the dough in half, patting it down gently. Repeat the process a couple of times until the dough is soft and cohesive. Wrap in plastic wrap and refrigerate at least 30 minutes or up to 24 hours.

Line a sheet pan with parchment paper. Return the dough to a lightly floured surface and re-roll into a disk about ½ inch thick. Using a 1 ½ inch-wide round biscuit or cookie cutter and pushing straight down, cut out as many biscuits as possible and arrange on the sheet pan, leaving 1 inch between them. You should have at least 24 biscuits. Place the pan of biscuits in the refrigerator for 15 minutes.

While the biscuits are chilling, preheat the oven to 400°F. Bake biscuits until lightly browned on top and baked through.

Tear the ham slices into two or three pieces per slice and fold in half so that they will fit inside the biscuits. Slice each biscuit in half. Brush each cut side with the melted butter. Place a piece of ham on the bottom half of each side and smear the preserves or jelly on the top half. Combine and serve immediately.

Grillades

hen I lived in Washington, D.C., and Manhattan, a big pot of grillades, always accompanied by a casserole of cheese grits, was one of my Sunday dinner-party staples. Homey but marked by complex spices and deep flavor, grillades are the ultimate in sophisticated comfort food. They are also the perfect brunch dish for hungry revelers. As is so often the case, the late, great Paul Prudhomme was my guide here. He insisted on seasoning the meat as well as the flour it is dredged in. That double whammy, as well as the initial browning, is what gives the dish its memorable character. During the cold-weather months, there's always a batch in my freezer.

In a small bowl, thoroughly blend the first eight ingredients and ½ teaspoon of the thyme to create your seasoning mix and set aside. (You won't need all of it.)

Sprinkle about 2 teaspoons of the mix all over the meat. In a sheet pan, combine ½ cup of the flour with another teaspoon of seasoning mix. Dredge the meat in the flour and shake off the excess.

Heat the oil in a large deep skillet or Dutch oven and fry the meat until golden brown, 2 to 3 minutes per side. Transfer the meat to a plate or another sheet pan and leave the oil in the skillet over high heat.

Sprinkle in the remaining ½ cup of flour, whisking constantly. Continue whisking until the roux is a medium brown, about 3 minutes. Immediately dump in the chopped vegetables and garlic and stir with a wooden spoon until well blended. Add the bay leaves and another 2 teaspoons of seasoning mix. Continue cooking for 5 minutes, stirring constantly.

Add stock to the vegetable mixture, stirring until well incorporated. Add the meat, wine, tomatoes, Worcestershire sauce, and thyme and bring to a boil. Reduce to a simmer, cook for about 20 minutes, and check for seasonings. Add seasoning mix to taste. Simmer until meat is tender and some pieces are falling apart, about another 20 minutes. Remove and discard bay leaves and serve hot, with Baked Garlic Cheese Grits Casserole (page 146).

1 tablespoon salt

1 ½ teaspoons onion powder

1 ½ teaspoons garlic powder

1 ½ teaspoons cayenne pepper

1 teaspoon white pepper

1 teaspoon sweet paprika

1 teaspoon black pepper

½ teaspoon dry mustard

1 ½ teaspoons dried thyme

2 pounds boneless veal or pork shoulder, cut into thin slices

1 cup all-purpose flour

¼ cup plus 3 tablespoons vegetable oil

1 cup chopped onions

1 cup chopped celery

1 cup chopped green bell peppers

2 teaspoons minced garlic

4 bay leaves

3 cups dark chicken or beef stock

½ cup red wine

1 ½ cups canned whole peeled tomatoes, drained and crushed by hand

1 tablespoon Lea & Perrins Worcestershire sauce

Baked Garlic Cheese Grits Casserole

Serves 8 to 10

8 tablespoons (1 stick) butter, plus more for greasing the dish

1 ½ cups quick-cooking (not instant) grits

2 cups grated sharp cheddar cheese

2 teaspoons minced garlic

½ cup finely chopped scallions, including the tender green parts

3 large eggs, lightly beaten

¾ cup whole milk

1 teaspoon Lea & Perrins Worcestershire sauce

¼ teaspoon cayenne pepper, or more to taste

Where I come from it is near blasphemy to admit this, but I despise grits—unless they are significantly souped up with sharp cheese, garlic, and cayenne, and scallions, too, for good measure. Then I can't get enough of them. This casserole is a crowd pleaser and the only accompaniment I have ever offered with grillades.

Preheat the oven to 375°F. Butter a 2-quart casserole dish.

Cook the grits according to the directions on the package. Remove from heat and add the butter, cheese, garlic, and scallions. Stir until both butter and cheese are melted and well incorporated. Whisk together the eggs and milk and stir into the grits along with the Worcestershire sauce and cayenne.

Pour the grits into the prepared dish and bake for 45 minutes to 1 hour, until the top is bubbly and slightly browned around the edges.

Grapefruit & Avocado Salad

My mother has served this salad every Christmas since I can remember, probably because someone always gives us a crate of Ruby Red grapefruits from Texas. It's one of my favorites and a bright counterpoint to rich and stewy foods like those on offer here. It looks really pretty as a sort of semi-composed salad on a fancy platter. But if I am feeling lazy or if I have a big crowd, I just toss all of the ingredients in a bowl.

In a small bowl, combine the lemon juice and the vinegar with the mustard and salt. Whisk in the oils and set the dressing aside.

Cut between the membranes of the peeled grapefruits to release the segments. Place on a large plate or rimmed sheet pan. You may do this a few hours ahead of time if you keep the segments covered and refrigerated.

When ready to serve, separate the lettuce leaves and trim where need be. Set aside some of the prettiest outer leaves to line the platter. Peel and pit the avocados and cut them into ¼-inch slices.

Place the reserved lettuce leaves in a large salad bowl and toss with just enough dressing to coat very lightly. Arrange around the edge of your serving platter. Place the remaining lettuce in the bowl and add the grapefruit segments, avocado, onion, and black pepper to taste. Toss with the dressing and taste for seasoning. Pile in the center of the platter and serve immediately.

1 tablespoon freshly squeezed lemon juice, plus more for the avocados

1 tablespoon sherry wine vinegar

1 teaspoon Dijon mustard

½ teaspoon salt

¼ cup extra-virgin olive oil

¼ cup vegetable oil

3 pink or Ruby Red grapefruits, all peel and pith cut away

2 heads Boston lettuce or Romaine hearts, or one of each

3 ripe avocados

1 small red onion, thinly sliced

Freshly ground black pepper to taste

MENU

BLACK VELVET / IRISH KISS

PAN-FRIED OYSTERS
with Salmon Pearls

CRAB PUDDING SOUFFLÉS
with Cashel Blue Sauce

SLOW-ROASTED LAMB SHOULDER
with Honey & Herbs

WARM POTATO SALAD
with Charred Cabbage,
Watercress & Peas

ORANGE BREAD PUDDING
with Irish Whiskey Sauce

An Elegant St. Patrick's Day Lunch

The Irish have been part of the fabric of New Orleans pretty much from the get-go—the first documented celebration of St. Patrick's Day in the city was in 1806, just two and a half years after the Louisiana Purchase. But in the 1830s, an especially large wave of Irish immigrants arrived in the city to dig the New Basin Canal and they settled primarily on a strip of land adjacent to the Mississippi River, known ever after as the Irish Channel. Each year, the Irish Channel St. Patrick's Day parade rolls from the Channel through the Garden District and back, beginning and ending at the legendary Parasol's bar. But it is hardly the only activity. All day long, block parties occur at both Parasol's and Tracey's. (It's a short walk along Third Street from one to the other.) A smaller parade, organized by the legendary Molly's at the Market bar, rolls in the French Quarter (though usually a day earlier than the Channel parade, which rolls on the Saturday before St. Pat's), along with another put on by the Downtown Irish Club. In the Channel parade, which is the largest, 1,200 men dressed in tails or tuxedoes march with around thirty floats. Riders are given three bags of cabbage containing thirty heads each and these are tossed into the flamboyantly attired crowd—along with beads, "to-go cups," coins, and potatoes.

For our intimate St. Patrick's Day lunch, Sara and Paul Costello and I decided to stage a slightly more elegant affair in the Costellos' gorgeous green garden, so that we could fortify ourselves with some civilized food and drink before plunging into the raucous crowds. From our table behind the wrought-iron fence, we could hear all of the nearby goings-on, which made the party all the more festive. I am not at all averse to the earthy charms of corned beef and cabbage, but I decided instead to pay tribute to what I call the four major food groups of Ireland: oysters, crab, salmon, and lamb. Since all four are among my very favorite things, my well-being always soars when I'm across the pond, a state of affairs possibly also attributable to the large quantities of black velvet cocktails and Irish whiskey that I manage to consume. Given the holiday, we did not stint on the beverages either, offering no less than two cocktails and Champagne before we even sat down.

In keeping with the spirit of the day, I dressed up our table with my mother's Waterford goblets and pots of green and purple oxalis (otherwise known as the "sham-rock plant"). After the final bite of pudding, we toasted to a year of good luck and hit the cabbage-strewn streets.

Riders are given three bags of cabbage containing thirty heads each and these are tossed into the flamboyantly attired crowd—along with beads, "to-go cups," coins, and potatoes.

Black Velvet

Serves 1

4 ounces (½ cup) Champagne
4 ounces (½ cup) Guinness stout

I fell in love with the Black Velvet on my first trip to Ireland many moons ago, but it was actually invented in London at Brooks's Club on St. James's Street in 1861. Prince Albert, Queen Victoria's prince consort, had died, and it is said that a club steward meant the color of the drink to symbolize the black-and-purple armbands worn by mourners. Maybe so, but there is nothing mournful about this cocktail—the creamy Guinness mixes brilliantly with the dry, effervescent Champagne to make the ideal "daytime" drink.

Fill a Champagne flute halfway with Champagne. Carefully and slowly top with the Guinness.

Irish Kiss

The incredibly talented Christiaan Rollich heads up the cocktail program at Chef Suzanne Goin's Lucques Group of restaurants, which includes my favorite Los Angeles restaurants, Lucques, A.O.C., and Tavern. Christiaan makes his own bitters and syrups (and sometimes even the booze itself), scours farmer's markets for seasonal produce, and comes up with complex but perfectly balanced cocktails that are invariably tasty as hell. On Sunday nights, you can find him behind the bar at Lucques, where he comes up with a special cocktail to pair with the pre-set three–course Sunday supper. When I'm in L.A., I always make a point to pop in, but thankfully Christiaan is also generous with his recipes, as he was with this delicious St. Patrick's Day creation.

1 ½ ounces (3 tablespoons) Irish whiskey (Christiaan uses Jameson)

1 ounce (2 tablespoons) freshly squeezed lemon juice

¾ ounce (1 tablespoon plus 1 ½ teaspoons) Rosemary Stout Syrup (recipe follows)

1 ounce (2 tablespoons) stout

Rosemary sprig

Place whiskey, lemon juice, syrup, and stout in a shaker without ice and shake vigorously for 15 seconds. Add ice and shake again. Remove ice and give the cocktail one last vigorous shake.

Pour into a glass—I use a smallish juice glass while Christiaan uses a coupe. Garnish with the rosemary spring.

ROSEMARY STOUT SYRUP

Bring the stout and sugar to a boil in a medium saucepan over high heat. Cook until the sugar is completely dissolved, 4 to 5 minutes.

Remove from heat and allow the syrup to come to room temperature. Pour the syrup into a blender, add the rosemary leaves, and blend until the leaves are pulverized. Strain through a fine mesh sieve.

Makes about 2 cups

8 ounces (1 cup) stout (Christiaan prefers Old Rasputin)

8 ounces (1 cup) sugar

Leaves from 1 rosemary sprig

Pan-Fried Oysters with Salmon Pearls

Serves 6 to 8 as hors d'oeuvres

½ cup corn flour or Zatarain's
   Wonderful Fish Fri
   (unseasoned)
½ cup all-purpose flour
½ teaspoon salt
¼ teaspoon white pepper
24 fresh oysters, drained
2 tablespoons butter
2 tablespoons vegetable or
   canola oil
Watercress leaves
Buttermilk Dressing
   (recipe follows)
4 to 6 ounces salmon roe

Makes about 1 ½ cups

½ cup mayonnaise,
   preferably homemade
¼ cup heavy cream
2 tablespoons Dijon mustard
2 tablespoons freshly squeezed
   lemon juice
1 tablespoon minced chives
   (optional)
½ cup buttermilk
Kosher salt to taste
Tabasco sauce to taste

Since oysters are at least as plentiful (and beloved) in Ireland as they are in New Orleans, they were a must for our menu. And though salmon is not exactly indigenous to our local waters, it might as well be Ireland's national fish, so I included a nod to the pink-fleshed beauty by using its roe as "pearls" atop our oysters. I also made a slightly more elegant version of that perennial favorite, ranch dressing, and accompanied the hors d'oeuvres with the appropriately named Billecart Salmon, my favorite rosé Champagne.

Mix the two flours, salt, and pepper in a small shallow pan suitable for dredging. Dredge the oysters in the flour, shaking off the excess, and place on a rimmed baking sheet lined with wax paper.

Heat the butter and oil in the skillet over medium-high heat until the butter is melted. Add only enough oysters to fit comfortably without crowding the pan. Cook until golden brown, less than 1 minute per side, and drain on paper towels (you can replace the wax paper on the baking sheet with paper towels and reuse it). Repeat until all the oysters are cooked, adding more butter and oil to the skillet if needed.

Place a watercress leaf or two in each indentation on an oyster plate and top with a hot oyster. Drizzle a bit of the dressing on top and garnish with a generous spoonful of salmon roe.

BUTTERMILK DRESSING

Combine all ingredients except the buttermilk, salt, and Tabasco in a bowl and mix well.

Whisk in the buttermilk until the dressing is smooth. Season with salt and Tabasco to taste.

NOTE: If you don't have oyster plates, you can serve these in the bottom halves of clean oyster shells placed on a platter, or just line a platter with watercress leaves and plop the oysters on top. I serve these, as hors d'oeuvres alongside a pile (or a pretty glass) of seafood forks and cocktail napkins so that people can help themselves.

Crab Pudding Soufflés with Cashel Blue Sauce

Makes 6 soufflés

4 tablespoons (½ stick)
*   butter, plus more for*
*   greasing ramekins*
¼ cup all-purpose flour
1 ½ cups whole milk
1 ½ teaspoons salt
6 scallions, sliced, with some
*   of the tender green parts*
2 leeks, sliced, with some
*   of the tender green parts*
2 cloves garlic, sliced
½ cup grated sharp
*   Irish cheddar*
Cayenne pepper to taste
3 large eggs, separated
½ pound lump crabmeat,
*   picked over for*
*   shell and cartilage*
½ cup finely grated Parmesan
2 cups heavy cream
¾ cup crumbled Cashel blue
*   cheese, or other semisoft*
*   blue cheese*

Like oysters, crabs are plentiful in Ireland and super popular (though there, the majority of dishes are made of meat from the brown crab), so I decided to give our local blue crab an Irish twist by combining it with two of my favorite Irish cheeses. Several Irish cheddar brands are available in U.S. grocery stores, and Cashel blue, a semisoft farmhouse cheese that was the first Irish blue, is on offer at most cheese shops. In a pinch, use any good sharp cheddar and a similar semisoft blue. The great benefit of this appetizer is that while it is elegant and impressive (as well as seriously delicious), you can make it ahead of time and reheat it at the last minute.

Melt 3 tablespoons of the butter in a heavy-bottomed pan, over medium heat. Whisk in the flour and cook for 3 to 4 minutes, stirring to keep the bottom from browning. Slowly pour in the milk, a little at a time, whisking after each addition until smooth before adding more. Add ½ teaspoon of the salt, reduce heat to very low, and cook, stirring frequently, until the béchamel is medium thick and free of lumps, about 20 minutes. Set aside to cool.

Melt the remaining 1 tablespoon of butter in a skillet or sauté pan over medium heat and add the scallions and leeks. Cook for about 4 minutes. Turn down the heat to low, and stir in the garlic and 1 teaspoon of salt. Stir in a splash (about 1 tablespoon) of water (to keep vegetables from browning) and cook until the water has evaporated, about 5 more minutes.

Remove from heat and allow to cool for a few minutes, then transfer the vegetables to a food processor fitted with a steel blade. Pulse until pureed and stir the puree into the béchamel. Add the cheddar and a pinch of cayenne, and mix well. Taste for seasonings—the mixture should be pretty highly seasoned. Add the egg yolks, lightly beaten, and mix well. Gently fold in the crabmeat.

Preheat the oven to 400°F.

Generously butter six 8-ounce ramekins. Dust the inside of each with the Parmesan, shaking out the excess.

In a medium bowl, beat the egg whites until they have soft peaks and then fold them into the crab mixture. Fill the ramekins with the crab mixture and sprinkle the tops with any remaining Parmesan.

Place the ramekins in a deep baking dish and pour enough hot water into the baking dish to reach halfway up the sides of the ramekins. Bake, until the soufflés are puffed and golden brown on top, 20 to 30 minutes. Carefully remove the ramekins from the hot water. When the soufflés have cooled a bit, run a knife around the edge of each ramekin, invert the soufflé into the palm of your hand, and place in a baking dish right side up. At this point the soufflés can be held at room temperature for a few hours.

When ready to serve, preheat the oven to 425°F and make the sauce. Heat the heavy cream in a saucepan over medium heat until barely bubbling and stir in the crumbled blue cheese. Stir frequently until the cheese has melted and is well incorporated. Keep warm over very low heat.

Put the soufflés in the oven and bake until they are hot and puffed up again, 6 to 8 minutes. Place on individual plates and pour some of the blue cheese sauce around them. Serve immediately.

Slow-Roasted Lamb Shoulder with Honey & Herbs

Serves 6 to 8

I have loved lamb since I was a tiny child and my grandmother's cook made a lovingly caramelized leg that was my favorite dinner. That memory and the memory of a long-ago Sunday lunch in London inspired this roasted lamb shoulder. At the lunch, a dear friend's Australian beau served us a leg that had been glazed with honey in his very swell Chelsea town house, and I remember being surprised and then delighted by the unexpected combo. Here, I use a lamb shoulder. (It's not always easy to find, but D'Artagnan

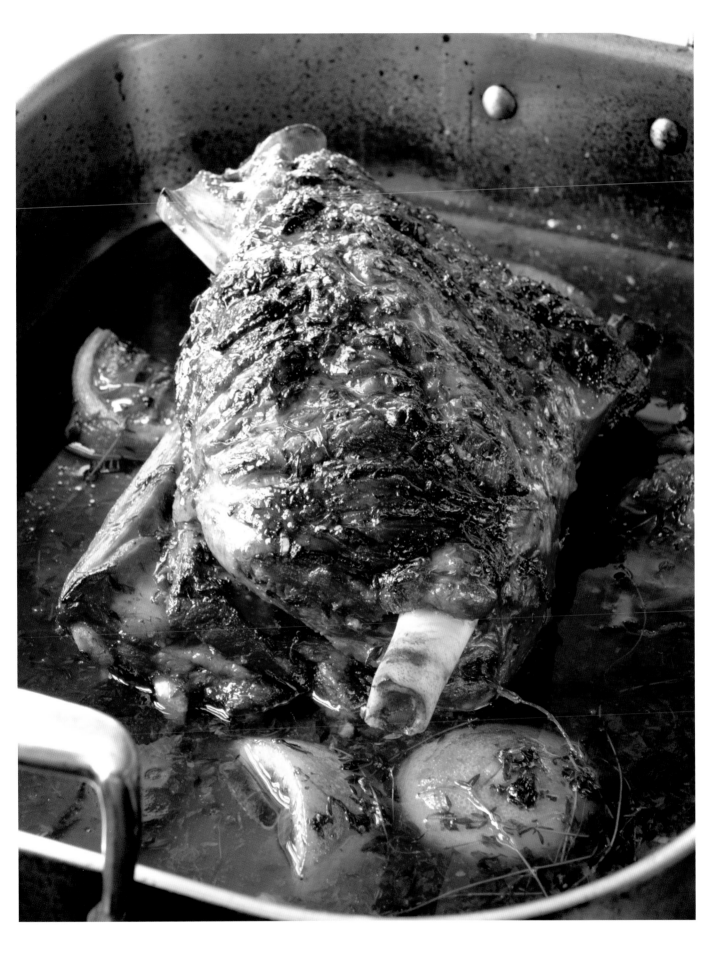

1 bunch fresh thyme

One 6-pound bone-in
lamb shoulder

8 tablespoons (1 stick) butter

½ cup honey

Juice of 1 lemon
(save the juiced halves)

6 cloves garlic, crushed

1 tablespoon kosher salt

1 tablespoon Lea & Perrins
Worcestershire sauce

1 teaspoon Tabasco sauce

2 tablespoons finely chopped
tarragon leaves

2 tablespoons finely chopped
mint leaves

Freshly ground black pepper to
taste

Chicken stock or white wine
(enough to fill your pan by
1 ½ inches)

will ship you one overnight; see Sources on pages 218–19.) I love how the cut's generous intramuscular fat mixes with the sweet/tart marinade to make the same caramelized meat of my youth. The shoulder is also a forgiving cut, made for slow roasting or braising and almost impossible to overcook. Also, while I know lamb and rosemary go hand in hand, I decided to make use of thyme and some soft herbs instead. If you are a rosemary lover, by all means substitute it for the thyme—just be sure to chop the leaves before adding them to the butter marinade.

Preheat the oven to 475°F.

Pull enough leaves off the thyme sprigs to make 3 teaspoons and spread the remaining sprigs in the bottom of a heavy roasting pan. Dry the lamb well and score the top layer of fat in a crisscross pattern with a sharp knife.

Melt the butter in a saucepan over medium heat and add the honey, stirring until it is well incorporated. Add the lemon juice, garlic, salt, Worcestershire sauce, Tabasco, thyme leaves, tarragon, and mint. Stir and remove from heat.

Rub the marinade all over the lamb on both sides. Cut the spent lemon halves in half again and toss them on top of the thyme branches in the roasting pan. Place the lamb on top, fat side up, and season with black pepper. Cover with foil and place in the oven. Immediately turn the temperature down to 325°F.

Roast for 2 hours, then remove the pan from the oven, and pour in enough stock or wine to fill the pan by 1 ½ inches. Scrape some of the drippings from the bottom of the pan. Leave the pan uncovered and roast until the lamb is brown and crispy on top, about 30 additional minutes.

Warm Potato Salad with Charred Cabbage, Watercress & Peas

Serves 6 to 8

1 ½ pounds fingerling potatoes,
    cut in half lengthwise,
    or small yellow
    new potatoes, halved
¼ cup plus 2 tablespoons olive
    oil, plus more for tossing
Kosher salt to taste
Freshly ground black pepper to
    taste
1 cup frozen peas
½ large head green cabbage
1 bunch scallions, sliced about
    ¼ inch thick, with some of
    the tender green parts
½ cup watercress leaves
2 tablespoons mint leaves
1 tablespoon champagne
    vinegar

This recipe is an homage to those classic Irish potato dishes, champ and colcannon. Both are made with mashed potatoes and a ton of butter. Scallions (and sometimes green peas) are added to champ, while colcannon gets cabbage or kale with leeks, onions, or scallions. I love them both, but to me, they taste best in cooler months—plus there is plenty of richness going on in this menu.

Preheat the oven to 450°F. Toss the potatoes in a large bowl with 2 tablespoons of the olive oil, a generous pinch of salt, and a couple of grindings of black pepper. Arrange the potatoes, cut sides down, on a rimmed baking sheet. Roast until potatoes are browned on the cut sides, about 20 minutes. Use tongs to turn the potatoes over and roast until deep golden and tender, 8 to 10 more minutes. (Check the potatoes a couple of times after you turn them, because the timing really depends on their size.)

While the potatoes roast, cook the peas according to package instructions. Drain and set aside. Remove bruised outer leaves from the cabbage half and cut into 1-inch-wide slices (leave the core to help hold the slices together—you can cut it out later). Toss with 2 tablespoons olive oil, the scallions, and a pinch of salt. Heat 2 more tablespoons of the oil in a large, heavy-bottomed skillet over medium-high heat (if you have a cast-iron pan, now is the time to use it). Cook the slices 8 to 10 minutes on each side, turning as needed. Repeat until all the cabbage is done. As soon as the slices are cool enough to handle, roughly chop into 1- to 1 ½-inch pieces, discarding the core bits. Place in a large bowl with any remaining scallions you've scraped from the pan.

Add the potatoes to the cabbage and toss. Add the peas, watercress, mint, and vinegar and toss again. At this point, you should taste to see if more oil, vinegar, salt, and/or pepper are needed. Make the adjustments and serve slightly warm.

Orange Bread Pudding with Irish Whiskey Sauce

Serves 8 to 10

Bread pudding might be New Orleans's most beloved dessert. Commander's Palace is rightly famous for its bread pudding soufflé with warm whiskey cream, and the version at the Bon Ton Café (with raisins and a whiskey sauce) has tens of thousands of fans (and almost as many copycats). I find a lot of local puddings a tad on the sludgy side and prefer the English and Irish versions, which are a bit more custardy, as they contain more eggs and cream. In her cookbook, the Duchess of Devonshire (or more likely, her cook) called for a layer of marmalade on top. The hefty dose of orange zest included here is my nod to the marvelous Debo. For the sauce (and in the pudding, too), I use Redbreast or Green Spot, which are my favorite Irish drinking whiskeys by far. Their notes of soft fruit and molasses greatly enhance the proceedings.

In a large mixing bowl, whisk together the eggs, cream, milk, sugar, whiskey, vanilla, orange zest, nutmeg, and a generous pinch of salt. Stir in the bread cubes, making sure all are coated with the liquid. Let the mixture rest for about 20 minutes.

Meanwhile, preheat the oven to 350°F.

Butter a large baking dish. Pour in the bread mixture, smoothing the top. Bake until crispy around the edges and golden, 40 to 45 minutes. Allow the pudding to cool for about 15 minutes and serve warm with the warm whiskey sauce.

IRISH WHISKEY SAUCE

Melt the butter in a medium saucepan over medium heat until it begins to turn a light brown color, about 5 minutes, taking care that it doesn't burn. Stir in the sugar, corn syrup, cream, whiskey, vanilla, and a generous pinch of salt. Reduce the heat to low and simmer the sauce until it is thick enough to coat the back of a spoon.

8 large eggs

3 cups heavy cream

3 cups whole milk

1 cup sugar

⅓ cup Irish whiskey, preferably Redbreast or Green Spot

2 teaspoons pure vanilla extract

Grated zest of two navel oranges

1 teaspoon freshly grated nutmeg

Kosher salt to taste

5 cups 1- to 1½-inch cubes stale French bread

Butter for greasing dish

Irish Whiskey Sauce (recipe follows)

Makes about 2 cups

8 tablespoons (1 stick) butter

½ cup sugar

1 tablespoon light corn syrup

½ cup heavy cream

¼ cup Irish whiskey, preferably Redbreast or Green Spot

½ teaspoon pure vanilla extract

1 pinch kosher salt

MENU

APEROL SPRITZ

CHARCUTERIE PLATE

DONALD'S LEMON
ROSEMARY SHRIMP

MOSCA'S ICEBERG
CRAB SALAD

REBECCA'S TUMMALA

SPUMONI BOMBES

An Italian FEAST

Soundtrack for the cook: *Louis Prima,* "Sing, Sing, Sing"/ "I've Got the World on a String"

Between 1880 and 1910, tens of thousands of Sicilian and Southern Italian immigrants entered the United States through the Port of New Orleans and, thankfully, a great many stayed. So many settled in the lower French Quarter that at one point, it was known as Little Palermo. The immigrants cut sugarcane and ran truck farms, sold groceries and manufactured pasta, operated bars and restaurants. They not only put their own stamp on the existing Creole cuisine (which saw an almost immediate increase in the use of garlic), but also created a whole new style of Italian cooking. (Shrimp scampi, for example, evolved into barbecue shrimp.) They also brought yet another celebration to the city, this one to mark St. Joseph's Day, which honors the relief that St. Joseph provided during a famine in Sicily. The festivities take place on March 19, when the Italian American

Marching Club puts on a parade, and altars throughout the city overflow with lush offerings of food, flowers, medals, and figurines.

Many of the early Creole Italian restaurants still thrive—one of my favorite oyster bars in the city is at Pascal's Manale, though the restaurant is far more famous for the aforementioned barbecue shrimp. Manale's (as the locals call it) has been on the same corner of Napoleon Avenue (in a former grocery store purchased by Frank Manale) since 1913. Mandina's, the beloved Mid-City institution, also began as a grocery, opened by Sebastian Mandina in 1898, before morphing first into a pool hall and sandwich shop and then into a full-fledged restaurant in 1932. In 1905, Angelo Brocato began offering New Orleanians such exotica as *granita al limone* (now simply called lemon ice), cannoli, all manner of Italian cookies and cakes, and *torroncino,* a vanilla-based gelato with cinnamon and ground almonds. Those original creations and much more are all still available today at the Carrollton Avenue location, and these days, the company ships across the country as well.

The Italian Creole institution I head to most often is Mosca's, a short ride across the river from New Orleans in Westwego. An iconic roadhouse, complete with jukebox (stocked with hits by the likes of Louis Prima and Dean Martin), it was established in 1946 by Provino Mosca in a building owned by mobster Carlos Marcello, who became a regular. A winner of an America's Classics Award for regional cooking from the James Beard Foundation, it is now run by Mary Jo Mosca (who is also head chef) and her daughter, Lisa,

Not surprisingly, the heaping piles of food were met with some serious skepticism, but someone braved the first bite, and before the night was over both Naomi Campbell and Christy Turlington were enthusiastic converts.

and it still dispenses garlic-and-rosemary-scented sublimity on family-style platters. Among the must-haves on the menu are oysters Mosca, baked in an aluminum pie plate and topped with an ineffable crusty blend of bread crumbs and seasonings; shrimp Mosca, a delicious version of barbecue shrimp; "chicken à la Grande"; and spaghetti Bordelaise. Once, when a troupe of *Vogue* models (and makeup artists and hairdressers and fashion editors) were in town for a shoot, I took them there to dine. (The great photographer Arthur Elgort has excellent taste in all things and he insisted). Not surprisingly, the heaping piles of food were met with some serious skepticism, but someone braved the first bite, and before the night was over, both Naomi Campbell and Christy Turlington were enthusiastic converts.

The good news is that my dear friend Donald Link and his insanely gifted team, who have changed (and vastly improved) the culinary landscape of the city with five other superlative spots, have now opened Gianna, their own tribute to the city's Italian roots. The chef-partner at its helm is Rebecca Wilcombe, the former chef de cuisine at Herbsaint (where she won the 2017 James Beard Award for Best Chef in the South), who traveled with Donald and the gang on extensive research tours through the Italian countryside. The restaurant is named after Rebecca's grandmother (Gianna is also Rebecca's middle name), who lives in the Veneto region of Italy and has been a major influence on Rebecca's cooking. "My grandmother is an amazing cook and probably the main

reason for my love of food," Rebecca says. "I cook, because I love to eat. I love to eat, because I grew up surrounded by delicious food."

I am always surrounded by delicious food whenever I get with the group (including my festive friend, long-time general manager Heather Lolley, who is an owner of Gianna) that gathered in Donald's spacious home kitchen for our Italian feast. Rebecca made refreshing Aperol spritzes to accompany the yummy charcuterie plate from Cochon Butcher (featuring mortadella, salami, and pancetta, among other house-cured delicacies) and Donald cooked up skillet after skillet of his own take on scampi. By the time we dug into the gorgeous spumoni bombes, we were well sated, but we all wished we had pans of Rebecca's to-die-for tummala to take home.

Aperol Spritz

Ice cubes

3 ounces (⅓ cup) prosecco

2 ounces (¼ cup) Aperol

1 splash (½ teaspoon) soda
water

Garnish with 1 grapefruit peel,
about 1 inch wide and 2 inches long, or 1 slice

I t's no wonder this cocktail is one of the most popular aperitifs in Italy. Aperol is low in alcohol, aromatic, and citrusy, but not cloyingly sweet. It also happens to pair brilliantly with prosecco to make the perfect pick-me-up on a warm day—or pretty much any time. Rebecca enlivens a classic spritz by adding a slice of grapefruit or a wide strip of peel as a garnish rather than the usual orange slice. It is always served, she says, over ice, "lots of ice."

Fill a large wine glass or Collins glass with ice. Pour in the prosecco. (Adding it first keeps the Aperol from settling at the bottom.) Add the Aperol and top with a splash of soda water. Garnish with the grapefruit peel or slice.

Donald's Lemon Rosemary Shrimp

Serves 4 to 6 as hors doeuvres

Barbecue shrimp is part of the Creole Italian pantheon and is an undeniably delicious, albeit extraordinarily messy, dish. Popularized at Pascal's Manale, it almost always consists of shrimp still in their shells, showered with lots of rosemary, garlic, black pepper, and butter or oil or both, and baked in a cast-iron pan. Donald Link's sprightly riff on the classic allows the shrimp to shine, and by using a stovetop method, avoids the overcooking that so often mars the baked version. Warning: You should have at least another dozen shrimp on hand when you make this, as you're sure to want a second pan immediately.

Lay the shrimp on a dinner plate in a spiral pattern with the tails facing the outside of the plate. Sprinkle with the salt, paprika, pepper, herbs, and lemon zest on one side only.

Heat a cast-iron skillet over medium-high heat and add olive oil. When the oil begins to smoke slightly, slide the shrimp from the plate into the pan in one smooth motion. Hold the plate tilted toward the pan's left side and then pull the plate away to the right as you hold the shrimp in place so that they go into the pan in the same spiral pattern they were in on the plate.

After about 2 minutes, when the shrimp begin to turn pink on the bottom, flip them over with a spatula or tongs. Cook until they are a nice pinkish-red color on both sides, another 1 to 2 minutes. Finish with the lemon juice and remove from the pan onto a serving plate. Drizzle any oil and juices remaining in the pan over the shrimp.

12 shrimp, 16 to 20 count per pound, peeled with tails left on

⅛ teaspoon salt

⅛ teaspoon paprika

Scant ⅛ teaspoon freshly ground black pepper

¼ teaspoon chopped fresh rosemary

½ teaspoon chopped fresh oregano

Zest of 1 lemon

1 ½ to 2 tablespoons extra-virgin olive oil

Juice of 1 lemon

NOTE FROM DONALD:
Some Gulf shrimp are naturally salty. I like to taste one before I decide how much salt to use—a lot of the time, I end up not using salt at all. Also, make sure your shrimp are dry before seasoning them—and only season them right before you cook them. Otherwise, they will sweat and not get a good sear.

Mosca's Iceberg Crab Salad

Serves 6 to 8

1 large head iceberg lettuce

Juice of 1 lemon

Salt to taste

½ cup giardiniera, drained (I usually use the easy-to-find Mezzetta or Bella Famiglia brands)

½ cup Central Grocery's Italian Olive Salad (Central Grocery is a New Orleans shrine and worth visiting, but the salad is also available on Amazon)

Up to ½ cup olive oil

1 pound lump crabmeat, picked over for shells and cartilage

Freshly ground black pepper to taste

At the restaurant, this salad has three main ingredients—iceberg lettuce, lump crabmeat, and giardiniera. The latter, an Italian-style relish of pickled vegetables, lends the dish its official menu moniker, "Italian crab salad," but by any name, its bright, clean flavors make it addictive. I don't think I've ever been part of a table that didn't order a second bowl to share. Here, I add Central Grocery's Italian olive salad (a component of their iconic muffaletta sandwich) to the mix—its salty, oily goodness provides a terrific counterpoint to the giardiniera's vinegar. Get your ingredients together and consider this recipe a guideline—this is one of those things you really need to toss and taste. It might need a touch more oil or lemon. You might prefer another quarter cup of giardiniera or olive salad or both. Once you get your proportions down, you'll come back to this again and again, I promise. It's a perfect lunch or light supper on its own with some crusty French bread and a nice Italian white, or an easy prelude to a simple plate of pasta.

Tear or cut the lettuce into biggish bite-size pieces. Sprinkle with half the lemon juice and a hefty pinch of salt and toss. Add the giardiniera and the olive salad and toss again. The olive salad is packed in olive oil, but you will likely need more. Add as needed to lightly coat the lettuce—being careful not to overdress—up to about ½ cup. Add the crabmeat and the pepper and gently toss. I usually do this with my hands so as not to break up the crabmeat. Taste for seasoning. You may need more lemon juice and you will very likely need more salt. Serve immediately.

Rebecca's Tummala

A tummala is a traditional dish served on festive occasions in Sicily. Rebecca says her own tummala was inspired by a recipe she saw in an old Sicilian cookbook: "It seemed so homey and satisfying, yet sort of grand to me. It's a dish with so many ingredients, yet it's straightforward to make. There are other recipes for tummala that call for even more ingredients. Some have whole boiled eggs, peas, several kinds of meats, or even egg-and-cheese crusts." Maybe so, but with this one, Rebecca has achieved nirvana—it doesn't need another thing. Each of us left the table wishing we had one to take home to our freezer. It's the perfect thing to have on hand for special feasts or those days when you need a dose of some Italian grandmother–style love.

FOR THE STOCK AND THE CHICKEN

3 carrots

3 ribs celery

2 medium yellow onions

1 chicken, about 3 ½ pounds

2 cloves garlic

1 sprig rosemary

1 tablespoon whole black peppercorns

1 tablespoon salt

FOR THE RICE

4 ½ cups chicken stock (see above)

1 tablespoon salt

3 cups Arborio rice

TO MAKE THE STOCK AND THE CHICKEN

Cut the vegetables into large chunks and place in a large 12-quart pot with the chicken, garlic, rosemary, peppercorns, and salt. Add cold water to cover and bring to a near boil over high heat. As soon as the water looks like it is going to boil, reduce immediately to a gentle simmer and cook until chicken is cooked through and tender, about 1 hour and 15 minutes.

Remove the chicken and set aside to cool. Strain the broth and place 4 ½ cups in a smaller pot. Once the chicken is cool enough to handle, remove and discard the skin and bones and chop up the chicken meat. Set aside.

TO MAKE THE RICE

Bring the pot containing the 4 ½ cups of stock to a boil over high heat. Add the salt and the rice, and bring nearly to a boil. Stir the rice once, cover, and turn the heat to low. Cook for 10 minutes. Remove the pot from the heat and set aside, covered, to steam for 30 minutes. Leave covered until ready to use.

SEMISWEET GANACHE

Place the chopped chocolate in a medium bowl. In a small saucepan over medium heat, bring the heavy cream to a low boil. Pour the cream over the chocolate and whisk until completely combined.

Remove the frozen pistachio gelato from the molds and place on a wire rack over a large rimmed sheet pan. Pour the ganache over each bombe. Return the bombes to the freezer until ready to serve.

8 ounces semisweet chocolate (preferably 60 to 66 percent), roughly chopped
1 cup heavy cream

NOTE: Maggie's gelato is, of course, delicious, but in a pinch, you could fill the molds with Angelo Brocato's Sicilian Pistachio Nut Gelato or Talenti's Sicilian Pistachio. Just be sure and let them soften a bit first and don't forget the cherries.

The Classics.

Soundtrack for the cook: *Professor Longhair*, "Jambalaya"; *Jon Batiste*, "Redbeans"

Obviously, there are plenty of New Orleans "classics" spread throughout this book, from grillades and gumbo to a Ramos gin fizz and "Rockefeller" spinach. But no New Orleans cookbook would be complete without a nod to red beans and rice and the oyster loaf, or to such newer classics as a satsuma margarita and the inventive sandwich creations of Chef Mason Hereford at Turkey and the Wolf. In this chapter, I pay tribute to everything from my favorite local oyster bars and an iconic restaurateur to some of the tunes that best define the city's soul. The "Big Easy" (a term rarely used by locals) is often anything but—our many crosses to bear range from a perpetually high crime rate to potholes aplenty (I once broke my elbow crossing the street). The following people, places, and pretty perfect eats are among the many magical things that make living here worthwhile.

Chicken, Andouille & Tasso Jambalaya

1 ½ teaspoons salt

1 teaspoon cayenne pepper

1 teaspoon white pepper

1 teaspoon freshly ground
    black pepper

1 teaspoon chili powder

1 teaspoon paprika

1 teaspoon dried thyme

¼ teaspoon dried sage

2 tablespoons butter

2 tablespoons vegetable oil

2 pounds boneless, skinless
    chicken thighs, cut into
    3-inch pieces (you may
    also use a mix of thighs
    and breasts)

½ pound tasso, chopped

½ pound andouille sausage cut
    into ½-inch slices

1 ½ cups finely chopped onion

1 cup finely chopped green
    bell pepper

1 cup finely chopped celery

1 jalapeño, seeded and minced

1 tablespoon minced garlic

2 cups canned crushed tomatoes

1 tablespoon tomato paste

2 bay leaves

2 cups white rice

3 cups chicken stock

1 bunch scallions, finely
    chopped

Jambalaya is a Cajun classic that has achieved great popularity in New Orleans, especially around Mardi Gras and Jazz Fest— or any time you need to feed a hungry crowd. It's a forgiving dish—I've thrown in everything from leftover steak to oysters (but only in the last few minutes of cooking for the latter)—and it's an easy recipe to double or triple (though don't increase the pepper until the end, after you've had a taste). The combination of tasso (a spicy cured pork shoulder; see Sources on pages 218–19) and andouille sausage gives this particular version depth and a bit of heat. Served with a big salad and crusty French bread, it's the perfect laid-back party dish.

Preheat the oven to 350°F.

Mix the first eight ingredients in a small bowl to make the seasoning mix and set aside.

In a large, heavy-bottomed, oven-proof pot, melt the butter and oil over medium-high heat and brown the chicken pieces, 1 to 2 minutes per side. Remove the chicken from the pan and add the tasso and andouille and cook until the meat starts to brown, about 3 minutes. Add the onions and the reserved seasoning mix, stirring and scraping the bottom of the pot to incorporate any browned bits.

Cook for about 3 minutes, then stir in the green peppers, celery, jalapeño, and garlic. Cook for another 3 minutes, stirring frequently.

Add the crushed tomatoes, tomato paste, and bay leaves, and return the chicken to the pot. Bring to a simmer. Stir in the rice and stock, mixing well, and turn heat to high. When the mixture comes to a boil, remove from heat and cover the pot. Transfer to the preheated oven and cook until rice is tender but still firm and the liquid has been absorbed, 30 to 35 minutes. Before serving, remove the bay leaves and stir in the finely chopped scallions.

Crawfish Maque Choux

Serves 8

I first encountered maque choux, a South Louisiana dish with Native American roots, at Uglesich's, the late, great, and much-lamented New Orleans restaurant owned by Anthony and Gail Uglesich. Pretty much every dish that came out of that improbably tiny kitchen was life altering (and I'm not exaggerating, not even a little). Even this seemingly simple sauté was enhanced by the addition of crawfish tails—along with whatever ineffable magic Gail's touch invariably provided. I've tried to come close to their recipe here, but you can certainly leave out the crawfish. Donald Link serves his version (sans the tails) atop fried green tomatoes; he's also not averse to crumbling a bit of bacon into the mix (in that case, fry the bacon first and use the grease for sautéing the vegetables). This is great when both corn and tomatoes are at their peaks, but it's still pretty swell with frozen corn and canned tomatoes. I often make crawfish maque choux part of my Thanksgiving menu. Dried corn was served at the first Thanksgiving, after all, generously provided by our original Native American hosts, and the pilgrims foraged for shellfish.

3 tablespoons butter

1 onion, finely chopped

1 green bell pepper, finely chopped

1 jalapeño, seeded and minced

1 1/2 teaspoons salt

1/2 teaspoon freshly ground black pepper

Cayenne pepper to taste

3 cloves garlic, minced

1 cup tomatoes, peeled, seeded and chopped (if ripe, tasty tomatoes are not available, used canned whole peeled tomatoes, seeded and chopped)

2 cups corn, fresh or frozen

1/2 cup heavy cream

1 pound crawfish tails

Melt the butter in a large skillet over medium heat and add the onion, green pepper, jalapeño, salt, black pepper, and cayenne. Sauté, stirring frequently, for 5 minutes.

Raise the heat to medium high and stir in the garlic, tomatoes, corn, and heavy cream. When the mixture comes to a boil, lower to a simmer and cook until the corn is tender, about 10 minutes. Stir in the crawfish tails and cook until they are warmed through. Taste for seasoning and serve.

Red Beans and Rice

1 pound (2 cups) dried kidney
　beans (Camellia brand is
　by far the best)
2 tablespoons butter
2 cups finely chopped celery
2 cups finely chopped
　yellow or white onion
2 cups finely chopped green
　bell pepper
1 tablespoon minced garlic
4 bay leaves
2 teaspoons dried thyme
1 teaspoon dried oregano
1 teaspoon salt
½ teaspoon cayenne pepper
½ teaspoon freshly ground
　black pepper
½ teaspoon white pepper
3 smoked ham hocks
1 pound andouille sausage cut
　into ½-inch to ¾-inch slices
Cooked white rice
1 bunch scallions, finely
　chopped

Red beans and rice and Mondays are inextricably linked in New Orleans. Monday was traditionally wash day in the city, and the beans—enriched by Sunday's ham bone—could simmer unattended on the stove for hours while the women hand-scrubbed the laundry. Even though wash day is no longer a thing, old habits die very, very hard in New Orleans and red beans remain a Monday special in restaurants all over town. It's a great dish any day, easily reheated and suitable for crowds. Louis Armstrong said he considered red beans his "birthmark"—his recipe resides with his papers at Queens College and he frequently signed his letters "Red Beans and Ricely Yours."

Place the beans in a bowl and add cold water to cover by at least 2 inches. Let stand for at least 8 hours.

In a large, heavy-bottomed pot or Dutch oven, melt the butter over medium heat and add the celery, onion, green pepper, garlic, bay leaves, and seasonings, and cook for 8 minutes, stirring frequently.

Add the ham hocks and 8 cups of water. Raise the heat and bring to a boil. Lower to a simmer and cook for 15 minutes. Drain the soaked beans. Then add the beans and another 2 cups of water and bring to a boil.

Reduce the heat to a simmer and cook for 1 hour, stirring often. Remove the ham hocks, and set aside to cool.

Add the sausage and cook for another 45 minutes—at this point the beans should be breaking up a bit. Meanwhile, cut the meat off the ham hocks and cut it into a small dice. Stir the ham into the beans and cook for 15 minutes. Remove and discard bay leaves. Serve over rice and garnish with scallions.

CONSIDERING
the ✠OYSTER

ysters are to New Orleans what lobster is to Maine—the most immediately recognizable symbol of our culinary DNA. Plump, sweet, and mild (due to the freshwater influence of the Mississippi), Gulf bivalves are served in po'boys and on fried seafood plates, in gumbo and in oyster dressing, with all manner of toppings, including Rockefeller and Bienville, and threaded with crispy bacon en brochette as part of Galatoire's famed Grand Goute platter. A ton of folks swear by the broiled oysters at Drago's, but to me, they're not much more than delivery systems for garlic and butter and bread crumbs—which is not necessarily a bad thing, but the oyster is not allowed to shine. The best version of "broiled" oysters are from the wood-fired oven at Cochon, still plump and barely napped with sriracha butter. Like the great M. F. K. Fisher, whose title I have bastardized above, I will eat an oyster pretty much any way I can get it, but I love them best on the half shell in all their unadulterated glory. The spots listed on the next page serve the best.

CASAMENTO'S

4330 Magazine Street

Founded in 1919 and still owned by the same family, Casamento's remains tethered to the traditions of the last century, closing for almost four months each summer. Oysters on the half shell are usually slurped down at the stand-up bar while waiting in line for a table. Once seated, you might then proceed to an excellent fried shellfish platter (featuring impossibly light and crispy piles of oysters, shrimp, crab claws, catfish or trout fillets, and french fries) or my favorite oyster loaf in the city—served on thick slices of a Pullman loaf rather than the ubiquitous French bread. For the best of both worlds, order the half oyster, half shrimp—dressed, of course.

FELIX'S

739 Iberville Street

In his entire long life, my father has yet to make a trip to New Orleans that didn't begin with at least two dozen on the half shell from Felix's—, even before he bothers to check into his hotel. I'm not sure I've ever made it far enough inside to actually sit down at a table—there's no real reason to venture past the stand-up bar where the shuckers open oyster after oyster until you can eat no more. Conveniently located around the corner from Galatoire's (and next to my preferred parking garage), it's the perfect place to begin an epic meal: a half dozen (or more) from Felix's to whet the appetite, shrimp Yvonne or a lamb chop or two from Galatoire's, and a delicious boozy ice-cream drink from Mr. B's for dessert.

PASCAL'S MANALE

1838 Napoleon Avenue

Manale's, as it's invariably called by the locals, was founded in 1913 and has been famous for its barbecue shrimp since 1954. I prefer the barbecue shrimp po'boy (the shrimp is piled in a hollowed-out French loaf), but the dining rooms are a tad tired, as is much of the rest of the menu. The unsung gem of the place is the dark, wood-paneled lounge complete with long cocktail bar and cozy oyster bar tucked into a corner. It's open from 11:30 AM until 9 PM every weekday and until at least 10 PM on Saturdays. Lined with photos of famous diners, the room is a seductive spot in which to while away an afternoon—when there, I always feel like I'm slightly incognito in my own town.

PÊCHE SEAFOOD GRILL (PÊCHE)

800 Magazine Street

One of the gems in the empire so brilliantly run by Donald Link and Stephen Stryjewski, Pêche is helmed by James Beard Best Chef, South winner Ryan Prewitt (the restaurant was also named best new restaurant in the whole country that same year, in 2014). Chef Prewitt turns out exquisitely cooked whole fish with salsa verde, inventive tapas ranging from yummy shrimp toast to steak tartare with oyster mayo, and all manner of additional daily deliciousness. But the raw oysters are consistently the freshest, tastiest, and coldest in the city and absolutely not to be missed.

"The Peacemaker" Oyster Loaf

In the 1800s, an oyster loaf bore the nickname *la mediatrice* or "the peacemaker," because a late or errant husband would grab one from a French Quarter street vendor or an oyster bar to bring home to placate his angry wife. A regular fried oyster po'boy is made on New Orleans's typically squishy French bread and "dressed" with mayonnaise, shredded lettuce, and tomato. While I would never turn up my nose at one, I actually prefer the oyster loaf at Casamento's, which comes on two very thick pieces of toasted white bread. But to me, the holy grail—and the ultimate "peacemaker"—is a loaf that showcases the hot, crispy oysters by scraping out the crumb of the bread to create perfect crusty shells. I smear the shells with a coating of homemade tartar sauce, the French kind (rather than the too-sweet bottled American version riddled with pickle relish) and that's it. It is

heaven. Of course you could also dress the shells like a typical po'boy or smear them with ketchup-based cocktail sauce, as some folks do. You can't go wrong. But I am sticking by my own version of peace on a plate.

Preheat the oven to 350°F.

Slice the loaf or baguettes in half horizontally and remove the inside crumb, leaving ½-inch-thick shells. Place on a baking sheet.

Melt the butter in a small saucepan over medium heat. Add the garlic, parsley, and a pinch each of salt and cayenne. Cook the mixture for 2 to 3 minutes but do not allow the butter to brown. Remove the pan from heat and brush the insides of the shells with the butter mixture.

Drain the oysters. Spread the cornmeal on a cookie sheet and dredge the oysters, one at a time, shaking off any excess cornmeal. Place the oysters in one layer on a clean baking sheet or plate.

Bake the shells in the preheated oven for 7 to 10 minutes until they are golden.

Meanwhile, fry the oysters. Heat the vegetable oil in a deep skillet over medium-high heat until it reaches 350°F. (You can also check the temperature by sprinkling some of the cornmeal into the oil. If it spins and dances, the oil should be ready.) Gently drop an oyster into the hot oil. If it doesn't rise to the top, wait a minute or two and try again. If it does, add three or four more oysters, being careful not to crowd the pan. When the oysters are a light brown, remove them with a slotted spoon to paper towels to drain. Repeat with remaining oysters.

Spread the insides of the baked shells with the tartar sauce. Place the oysters in the bottom shell (or shells), sprinkle with salt and black pepper to taste, and cover with the top shell (or shells). If using one long loaf, cut the sandwich into four pieces. If using baguettes, cut them in half. Serve immediately.

1 loaf of French or Italian bread or 2 small baguettes

4 tablespoons (½ stick) butter

1 clove garlic, minced

1 tablespoon finely chopped Italian parsley

Salt to taste

Cayenne pepper to taste

1 pint fresh oysters, shucked

1 ½ cups white cornmeal or Zatarain's Wonderful Fish Fri (unseasoned)

4 cups vegetable oil

Homemade Tartar Sauce (recipe follows)

Freshly ground black pepper to taste

HOMEMADE TARTAR SAUCE

3 hard-boiled egg yolks

1 tablespoon Dijon mustard

½ teaspoon salt

1 cup vegetable, safflower,
    or canola oil

Freshly squeezed lemon juice to
    taste

¼ cup minced capers

3 tablespoons minced
    cornichons or dill gherkins

2 tablespoons finely chopped
    chives

1 tablespoon finely chopped
    Italian parsley

1 tablespoon finely chopped
    tarragon

Cayenne pepper to taste

Mash the egg yolks, mustard, and salt in a bowl until you have a smooth paste. Slowly drizzle in the oil, whisking constantly, until about one-third of the oil has been incorporated and the mixture is creamy. At this point, add the rest of the oil in a thin, steady stream, still whisking constantly. If the mixture gets too thick, add lemon juice as needed.

Stir in the capers and cornichons and mix well. Stir in the herbs and a pinch of cayenne and taste for seasoning. It may need more lemon, salt, or pepper.

Commander's Palace Whiskey Smash

Serves 1

3 lemon wedges

4 fresh mint leaves

1 ounce (2 tablespoons) orange
    Curaçao

2 ounces (¼ cup) bourbon

1 spring fresh mint

I first discovered the Whiskey Smash in 2007 when the two fabulous female proprietors of Commander's Palace, Ti Adelaide Martin and Lally Brennan, came out with their charmingly illustrated drinks book, *In the Land of Cocktails*. I was a tad late to the party, since the cocktail dates at least as far back as 1882, when it appeared in *Harry Johnson's New and Improved Bartender's Manual*. A more complex and citrusy version of a mint julep, the smash is an excellent hot-day libation.

Muddle the lemon wedges, mint leaves, and Curaçao in a bar glass or shaker. Add the bourbon and ice and stir or shake well. Strain into a rocks glass filled with ice and garnish with the mint sprig.

Satsuma Margarita

Like the original contributions to Creole cuisine, some of the more recent additions have happened organically. Mexican workers, thankfully, flooded the city after Katrina, and many of the food stands that opened across the city to feed them morphed into full-fledged restaurants. At El Gato Negro, the margaritas almost immediately acquired a Creole twist. In addition to limes, they are made with satsumas, loose-skinned, highly aromatic mandarin oranges that thrive in South Louisiana, and they are quite possibly the best margaritas I have ever had. Now that more than a decade has passed since its happy introduction, this addictive margarita has definitely earned "classic" status.

Add all ingredients to a mixing glass and shake or stir to mix well. Pour over ice in a highball or margarita glass.

1 ½ ounces white tequila (I use Patrón Silver)

1 ounce (2 tablespoons) freshly squeezed lime juice

4 ounces (½ cup) freshly squeezed Satsuma juice

1 ounce (2 tablespoons) Cointreau or triple sec

NOTE: To make a salted rim on the glass, spread a couple of tablespoons of kosher salt on a small plate. Rub one of the juiced lime halves around the edge of the glass and dip the rim into the salt.

Heaven in Your HANDS

6 of the City's Most Iconic Sandwiches with Their Makers

LOUISIANA SHRIMP ROLL

Ryan Prewitt, Pêche Seafood Grill
When Pêche opened in 2013, it showcased the same whole-animal cooking on offer at its nearby sister restaurant, Cochon, except that here it's nose to fin rather than nose to tail. The Louisiana shrimp roll is the only sand-

wich in the house, but believe me when I say that there need be no other. Prewitt has crafted the New Orleans version of that New England classic, the lobster roll—the Maine kind, featuring chunks of shellfish tossed with mayo and celery rather than the melted butter that marks the Connecticut roll. The dressed shrimp—a sweeter, saltier (and, in my admittedly biased opinion, way superior) substitute for lobster—is generously piled on a buttery, top-sliced bun fresh off the flat top and showered with shredded lettuce.

SLOW-ROASTED DUCK PO'BOY
Jack Leonardi, Crabby Jack's

At Jack Leonardi's much-loved flagship restaurant Jacques-Imo's, a grilled duck breast has long been on the menu. In 2002, when Leonardi opened Crabby Jack's, a lunch spot offering po'boys, gumbo, and other New Orleans favorites, he solved the problem of what to do with the leftover thighs by creating the city's greatest po'boy by far: one made with slow-roasted duck. The meat is braised in a huge, crusty cast-iron skillet, creating a crazy good "debris." "Debris" is the local term for falling-apart meat in a rich, garlicky, brown gravy, and here, it's further studded with bits of crispy duck fat and skin. These are fighting words in this town, but I never understood New Orleanians' tireless devotion to the po'boy—until I tasted this one.

RACHEL

Dan Stein, Stein's Market & Deli

Married actors Blake Lively and Ryan Reynolds met and fell in love on location in New Orleans while filming *The Green Lantern*. After the months-long shoot was over, they missed their favorite local sandwich so much they flew in from New York for an afternoon just to have one. Thankfully, Rachel nirvana is within walking distance for me, but I get it—I'd happily go a lot farther for Dan Stein's warm and crispy-edged pastrami served on rye with house-made coleslaw, Russian dressing, and melted Swiss, accompanied by my favorite house-cured pickles. Stein may hail from Philadelphia, but his superlative establishment hearkens back to the days when Jewish delis abounded in New Orleans. Stein's is traditional but also hip, offering delicious seasonal gazpacho along with restorative matzo ball soup and a vast craft beer selection. And then there's its irresistible unofficial motto: "Want a Po'boy? Go Somewhere Else."

VIETNAMESE ROASTED PORK BANH MI
Hai Le, Dong Phuong

After the fall of Saigon in 1975, New Orleans was among the handful of American cities that received a significant influx of Vietnamese refugees. Because the great majority were Catholic, Archbishop Philip Hannan took a lead role in resettlement, originally sponsoring 1,000 refugees, who settled in New Orleans East. Today, the population numbers more than 15,000, including dozens of restaurateurs who have made significant contributions to the city's culinary landscape. Since Vietnam had been occupied by the French from the late-nineteenth century until 1954, its baking culture blends nicely with that of New Orleans. Dong Phuong is among the Vietnamese bakeries that supply typically airy French bread to non-Vietnamese sandwich shops and restaurants all over town. Established in 1982 by De and Huong Tran, DP Bakeshop, as it is known, is among the most extensive in the city, offering everything from chocolate éclairs to traditional moon cakes. There's also a sit-down restaurant, but the banh mi counter is where the action is. The Vietnamese roasted pork version, otherwise known as the "Number 4," is one of the most popular of the seventeen varieties offered. Like the others, it comes dressed with the family's homemade aioli, julienned pickled carrots and daikon, sliced jalapeños, cucumbers, and fresh cilantro. Originally marketed as a "Vietnamese po'boy," the banh mi is now a beloved fixture in the city's sandwich firmament, as Hai Le, the maker pictured here, can proudly attest.

211

FRIED BOLOGNA

Mason Hereford, Turkey and the Wolf

Eyebrows might have been raised when *Bon Appétit* named a super-casual (mostly) sandwich joint located in a former filling station the best new restaurant of 2017, but the cooking at Turkey and the Wolf is anything but casual.. Owner Mason Hereford, who did time in the city's white-tablecloth restaurants, including the justifiably acclaimed Coquette, has an imagination that knows no bounds. This sandwich, a stunningly delicious riff on a white-trash childhood favorite, is a prime example. The bologna is locally made from pork raised on a Mississippi farm. The bread is homemade, too, thick sliced and butter griddled, smeared with Duke's (and only Duke's) mayo and homemade Engish mustard. Added to the mix is what Hereford insists on calling "shrettuce" (known to the rest of us as shredded iceberg), melted American cheese, and a pile of homemade potato chips that are brined in vinegar before being fried each morning. Once it's on the plate, "You crush it," he says. "You gotta make it so it'll fit in your mouth." The menu is full of equally swell stuff—the Reuben-like collard-green melt, also pictured here, is nothing short of astonishing—but if you're looking for a mouthful of nostalgic joy, the fried bologna is the thing. Says Mason, "Recapturing a childhood memory is a really effective way to convey what our food is and what inspires it."

COCHON MUFFALETTA
Donald Link,
Cochon Butcher

The muffaletta was invented in 1906 in the French Quarter's venerable Central Grocery (founded by Sicilian immigrant Salvatore Lupo), where it is still made today on enormous flat rounds of Italian bread topped with sesame seeds. One of my favorite lunches remains a Central Grocery quarter "muff," containing layers of Italian meats and cheese dressed with olive salad, accompanied by an ice-cold beer and consumed at the oil-rubbed wooden counters in the back of the store. As much as I love that original sandwich (which is now a fixture on menus all over town), leave it to my buddy Donald Link to make it better. Before Cochon Butcher opened in 2009, he worked for months to perfect his version: layers of house-cured mortadella, capicola, Genoa salami, and provolone cheese in perfect proportion to the house-made olive spread (green olives, carrots, and cauliflower with onion, garlic, oregano, and red wine vinegar). He also serves his hot: "It really brings out the meat and makes it nice and juicy, and I'm a sucker for melted cheese and meat." Enough said.

The Making of an Instant Classic: Fried Green Tomato with Shrimp Rémoulade

JoAnn Clevenger believes the idea to top a Deep South classic (the fried green tomato that was a delicacy of her North Louisiana childhood) with a Creole mainstay (the mustardy shrimp rémoulade of her adopted hometown) came to her in a dream. Whatever. The brilliant dish, added to Upperline's menu circa 1992 (just after the release of the film *Fried Green Tomatoes),* is now featured in restaurants across the country. New Orleans's late, great Uglesich's was among the first to pick it up (though the fried tomato slices were often replaced by mirliton, the pale green squash native to Louisiana); at Crabby Jack's the combo is a popular po'boy filling.

The dish is hardly the only classic at Upperline or, indeed, the only marriage of Deep South and Creole—the dark, andouille-flecked duck étouffée served atop perfect country cornbread comes immediately to mind. Clevenger opened the restaurant in 1982 after adventurous careers as a bar owner, flower-cart operator, and Broadway costumer. As a young French Quarter waitress, she mixed Dizzy Gillespie a cocktail when the white bartender refused to do so and they became fast friends. When she bought The Abbey bar, she was the first in the whole Southeast to offer Guinness on tap and the *New York Times* on Sunday mornings. More crucially, JoAnn was one of the first restaurateurs to reopen after Katrina—on that joyful October night, I saw people who said Upperline's comeback had been crucial to their own decisions to return to the city.

JoAnn has been a great mentor both to chefs and to artists, whose works line the walls of Upperline's cheery dining rooms. For the past few years, she has been a finalist for the James Beard Award for Best Restaurateur in the whole country. Though her competition always includes folks who preside over bigger operations in bigger cities, there is no one more deserving. JoAnn, in her signature red dress, presides over her rambling yellow clapboard empire with the warmth and humor of a Louisiana Auntie Mame. Dining with her is like being home, but better.

PLAYING the CLASSICS

"WALKING TO NEW ORLEANS"
Fats Domino

The great Bobby Charles says he wrote this song for Domino in fifteen minutes. It was recorded with Dave Bartholomew's backup band in Cosimo Matassa's legendary studio on Rampart Street. In the aftermath of Katrina, Domino's home in the Ninth Ward was flooded (he'd stayed in town because his wife was infirm) and the famed pianist was rumored dead, but he and his family were rescued by a Coast Guard helicopter and Domino died of natural causes in 2017. The song—performed by an unlikely Neil Young on *Goin' Home: A Tribute to Fats Domino*—became something of a post-Katrina anthem for folks trying to return to the city after the storm.

"DO YOU KNOW WHAT IT MEANS TO MISS NEW ORLEANS?"
Louis Armstrong and Billie Holiday

This song was first performed in the 1947 film *New Orleans,* a musical romance featuring Armstrong as a bandleader and Holiday as a singing maid. Their duet is pretty swell, as is Armstrong's subsequent solo version. For sheer New Orleans nostalgia, you can't beat the lyrics, with their images of "oleanders in June," "moonlight on the bayou," and the "lazy Mississippi hurrying into spring."

"CHECK MR. POPEYE"
Eddie Bo

Bo, who died in 2009, was a jazz and R&B pianist who was influenced by everyone from Art Tatum to Vladimir Horowitz and released more singles than any other New Orleans musician except Fats Domino. This song, first recorded in 1962, was a huge regional hit and kicked off one of the major dance crazes of the early sixties. Bo was also a carpenter with a successful renovation business. He was on tour in Paris when Katrina destroyed his house and studio, but he returned to rebuild both himself.

"WAY DOWN YONDER IN NEW ORLEANS"
Louis Armstrong and Bing Crosby

This song was written in 1922 by John Turner Layton and Henry Creamer and advertised as a tune "without a mammy, a mule, or a moon," a not-so-subtle dig at the clichéd Tin Pan Alley lyrics of the era. Harry Connick, Jr., sang a lovely version in the September 2005 NBC Katrina fundraiser, "A Concert for Hurricane Relief," which raised more than $50 million. But for unadulterated joy, you can't beat the recording by Louis Armstrong and Bing Crosby because they are so clearly having a ton of fun.

"St. James Infirmary Blues"
Snooks Eaglin

I first heard this song decades ago when my father took me to Bourbon Street's Famous Door (now, sadly, a tourist trap with uninspiring music). That night, the song was performed by an albino clarinetist named Hollis Carmouche and his orchestra. Daddy sang every word, and afterward an African American tap dancer he knew named Pork Chop came in and danced on the bar. As dour as the lyrics are, the song always brings happy memories of that festive night and it's often performed with an incongruously joyful beat. Of indeterminate origin, it has been recorded by everyone from Louis Armstrong and Cab Calloway to Joe Cocker and the White Stripes, but I especially like this version by the New Orleans—based blind blues guitarist Snooks Eaglin.

"Mother-in-Law"
Ernie K-Doe

This 1961 recording of an Allen Toussaint song by Ernie K-Doe (née Ernest Kador, Jr.) made it to number one on the *Billboard* pop chart and the singer traded on its success for the rest of his career. In the 1990s, he began performing in a cape and crown and billed himself "Emperor of the Universe." With his wife, Antoinette K-Doe, he also opened the Mother-in-Law Lounge, dominated by a life-size mannequin of K-Doe (put to use by Antoinette when she launched her late husband as a—sort of—tongue-in-cheek mayoral candidate just after Katrina). Antoinette died in 2009, but the club has thankfully been preserved by popular local musician Kermit Ruffins, who operates it as Kermit's Mother-in-Law Lounge.

"Red Beans (a.k.a. I Got My Mojo Working)"
Professor Longhair

Born Henry Roeland "Roy" Byrd in 1918, Professor Longhair is known for a piano style heavily inflected with rhumba and mambo beats. He enjoyed two heydays, first in the early R&B era, and again after the founding, in 1970, of the New Orleans Jazz and Heritage Festival and the subsequent resurgence of interest in traditional jazz. The great New Orleans music venue Tipitina's is named after one of the Professor's signature songs, and a bust of his likeness greets patrons inside the door. It's fitting that the club has no seating to speak of—I defy anyone to stay sitting down when listening to this song.

"Black Bottom Stomp/ New Orleans Joy"
The Dukes of Dixieland with Danny Barker

Both these infectious tunes are included in *Salute to Jelly Roll Morton,* a tribute to the pivotal early jazz pianist, who began his career in the city. When I first started spending time in the city, I once had the privilege of meeting Danny Barker, a rhythm guitarist and banjoist who played with the likes of Morton, Sidney Bechet, Charlie Parker, and countless other legends. The occasion was a 1991 *Vogue* photo shoot by Arthur Elgort in which Naomi Campbell and Christy Turlington posed with a delighted Barker on his front steps. In 1970, Barker founded the Fairview Baptist Church Marching Band (it later morphed into the Dirty Dozen Brass Band), which helped launch the careers of such future New Orleans greats as Branford and Wynton Marsalis, Nicholas Payton, and Dr. Michael White.

TABLETOP

Lucullus

610 Chartres Street
New Orleans, LA 70130
504-528-9620
lucullusantiques.com

Patrick Dunne has assembled an extensive collection of culinary antiques, from copper cookware and silver serving pieces to nineteenth-century stemware, oversize monogrammed napkins, and porcelain, including the gorgeous cornflower garland pattern used in the Restaurant Tribute chapter on page 43.

FOOD, WINE, AND SPIRITS

Beth Biundo Sweets

3917 Baronne Street
New Orleans, LA 70115
504-899-8059
bethbiundosweets.com

Big Fisherman

3301 Magazine Street
New Orleans, LA 70115
504-897-9907
bigfishermanseafood.com

Big Fisherman has delicious boiled crawfish to take out in season, but they'll also pack everything from frozen crawfish tails and crawfish pies to Louisiana shrimp and an assortment of local seasoning brands for travel or to ship.

Central Grocery

923 Decatur Street
New Orleans, LA 70116
504-523-1620
centralgrocery.com

Cochon Butcher

930 Tchoupitoulas Street
New Orleans, LA 70130
504-588-7675
cochonbutcher.com

D'Artagnan

800-327-8246
dartagnan.com

America's best and most comprehensive source for meat and poultry (including the Rohan ducks on page 119 and the bone-in lamb shoulder on page 164) as well as such all-important pantry items as veal demiglace and duck fat.

Keife and Co.

801 Howard Avenue
New Orleans, LA 70113
504-523-7272
keifeandco.com

Langenstein's

1330 Arabella Street
New Orleans, LA 70115
504-899-9283
langensteins.com

I have friends who drive many hours just to pick up containers of

Better Cheddar and Le Popeye dips. A beloved local institution, it's also my go-to for the best beef in town, pints of P&J oysters, and the freshest jumbo lump crabmeat.

Martin Wine Cellar
3827 Baronne Street
New Orleans, LA 70115
504-899-7411
martinwine.com

Poche's
3015 Main Highway
Breaux Bridge, LA 70517
800-376-2437
pochesmarket.com

My favorite source for Cajun specialty meats, from tasso and andouille to stuffed chickens and fresh chaurice, will ship anywhere in the country. But if you're in the neighborhood, stop in for the daily lunch specials, which include stuffed pork chops, red beans and rice, and crawfish étouffée.

P&J Oyster Company
1039 Toulouse Street
New Orleans, LA 70112
504-523-2651
oysterlover.com

St. James Cheese
5004 Prytania Street
New Orleans, LA 70115
504-899-4737

641 Tchoupitoulas Street
New Orleans, LA 70130
504-304-1485
stjamescheese.com

Sucré
3025 Magazine Street
New Orleans, LA 70115
504-520-8311
shopsucre.com

Index

ACKNOWLEDGMENTS

I am grateful for the day that Paul Costello and his wife, Sara, decided, like me, to make a permanent move from Manhattan to New Orleans. Since then, we have become neighbors, collaborators, and, best of all, close friends. I could not have done *Julia Reed's South* without Paul, who not only creates gorgeous images but is the best coconspirator and traveling companion a girl could have. Likewise, he brought *Julia Reed's New Orleans* to life. Sara and Paul also offered up their house and garden for both the St. Patrick's Day and Reveillon parties. Spending time in their magical space is always a gift.

Alex Darsey, Paul's sometime assistant, and a talented photographer in his own right, joined us for some of the shoots—and makes an appearance in the Aoili Dinner portrait. He is not only a tireless worker, he always adds to the fun. Laine Thomas, Paul's intrepid studio manager kept us super organized and contributed to the finished product in countless ways, large and small.

This is the third book I've had the pleasure of doing with Sandy Gilbert Freidus, my editor at Rizzoli. I owe Sandy an enormous debt for her enthusiasm and support, her sharp eye and deft pen, and, perhaps most of all, her monumental patience and fortitude. Sandy, you know I can never thank you enough.

The uber-talented Roberto de Vicq and his wife and partner, Fearn, are at this point the only designers I can imagine working with. They immediately "get" any project I throw their way. This book is theirs as much as mine and Paul's. And thank you again, Sandy, for having the good sense to put us together.

I also want to thank Charles Miers, publisher of Rizzoli, for embracing this project.

My dear friends Patrick Dunne, John D. and Melissa Gray, and Peter Patout opened their houses to me for this book, as they so often do in real life. All four should have their photos in *Webster's* next to the word "hospitality."

Everett Bexley, Lisa Rogers, Terrell Johnson, and Julie Trice provided invaluable help during the shoots for this book. Everett miraculously manages to keep my life on an even keel most days.

Chris Granger, the wonderful New Orleans–based photographer who captures the city so brilliantly for the New Orleans *Advocate* among other publications, supplied the photos of the festive Mardi Gras candids and me in the giant shoe, the Cochon Butcher king cake, and the St. Patrick's Day parade images.

I want to thank the George Rodrigue Foundation of the Arts for the use of the painting *Aioli Dinner*. The Foundation's own Aioli Dinner Supper Club benefits its mission to encourage the use of art in education.

My ever-generous friend John Alexander allowed the use of *Ballers,* his oil painting fittingly owned by Donald Link. The Link-Stryjewski Foundation puts on an annual Bal Masqué that is not to be missed.

The chefs who appear on these pages are not just heroes in my own life but contribute immeasurably to the life of the city. I especially want to thank Donald Link, Stephen Stryjewski, Heather Lolley, Ryan Prewitt, Rebecca Wilcombe, Emery Sonnier, Jason Goodenough, John Harris, Kristen Essig, Mason Hereford, Dan Stein, and JoAnn Clevenger. They are all incredibly supportive of all that I do. More important, they and their creations are pretty much the point of my incredibly blessed existence in my adopted city.

First published in the
United States of America in 2019
by Rizzoli International
Publications, Inc.
300 Park Avenue South
New York, New York 10010
www.rizzoliusa.com

⚜

Text © 2019 by Julia Reed
Photography © 2019
by Paul Costello,
with the exception of the following:

⚜

Alamy Stock Photo: page 175
IStock Photo: Casewrap
Shutterstock Photo: page 12

⚜

John Alexander's *Ballers* (courtesy
of the artist): pages 138–39

⚜

Christopher Granger:
pages 5, 133, 134, 137, 153

Library of Congress Prints and
Photography: Arnold Genthe:
pages 15, 67, 83, 151, and 191;
Frances Benjamin Johnston:
page 13; Frances Benjamin
Johnston (Carnegie Survey of the
Architecture of the South, Library
of Congress, Prints and Photographs
Division): pages 39, 103, 173

⚜

George Rodrigue's *Aioli Dinner,*
1971 (courtesy of George Rodrigue
Foundation of the Arts. The Aioli
Dinner Supper Club raises funds for
the Foundation, supporting the arts
in education in Louisiana.): page 85

⚜

2020 2021 2022/
10 9 8 7 6 5 4 3 2
Printed in Italy

⚜

ISBN 13: 978-0-8478-6364-8

⚜

Library of Congress
Control Number: 2018961291

⚜

PROJECT EDITOR:
Sandra Gilbert
ART DIRECTION & DESIGN:
de Vicq design
PRODUCTION: Alyn Evans
EDITORIAL ASSISTANTS:
Natalie Danford, Susan Homer,
Marilyn Flaig, Sara Pozesky